Adopting

**A
guide
for
people
interested
in
adoption**

Jenifer Lord

BAAF
ADOPTION
& FOSTERING

Published by
British Association for Adoption & Fostering
(BAAF)
Saffron House
6 – 10 Kirby Street
London EC1N 8TS
www.baaf.org.uk

Charity registration 275689

© BAAF 1984, 1986, 1990, 1995, 1998, 2002, 2005, 2006

© BAAF 2006

British Library Cataloguing in Publication Data
A catalogue reference record for this book is available from the
British Library

ISBN 1 903699 93 2

Photography by John Birdsall; www.johnbirdsall.co.uk and
www.istockphoto.com
All photographs posed by models
Designed by Andrew Haig & Associates
Typeset by Aldgate Press
Printed in Great Britain by Creative Print and Design Ltd.

Contents

Acknowledgements

The first four editions of *Adopting A Child* were co-authored by Prue Chennells and Chris Hammond in 1984, 1986, 1990 and 1995. Jenifer Lord made considerable revisions for the fifth edition in 1998, the sixth in 2002, and for this eighth edition in 2006.

This edition draws on the previous editions but contains new material and significant amendments in light of recent government initiatives and of legislative changes in England and Wales.

The author would like to thank Ian Millar, BAAF Scotland, for his helpful comments, particularly in relation to legislation and practice in Scotland; Katrina Wilson, BAAF, for her efficient help with statistical information; and Shaila Shah and Jo Francis in BAAF Publications for their hard work in producing this edition.

The quotations in this book have been taken from several sources:
Personal communication to the author
Adopted Children Speaking, BAAF, 1999
Looking after our Own, BAAF, 2005
Could you be my Parent?, BAAF, 2005
Supporting Adoption, BAAF, 1999
Staying Connected, BAAF 2002
Adoption Today, Adoption UK
Foster Care magazine, Fostering Network

Introduction

Almost 6,000 children were adopted in the year to March 2005 in the UK.* About two-thirds of these are children who have been looked after by a local authority. The others are predominantly children adopted by their parent and step-parent, and about 300 are children who have been brought from overseas and adopted by people living in the UK. There is a chapter in this book addressed to step-families considering adoption and one to people considering adopting from overseas. The rest of this book is about the adoption of children who are looked after by local authorities. There is also a chapter on meeting these children's needs through fostering.

There are currently almost 80,000** children looked after by local authorities in the UK, over two-thirds of them in foster homes. The majority of the total number of looked after children will return home to their family within a year.

Although the number of looked after children who are adopted has risen in recent years, it still represents a tiny proportion, just over 5 per cent, of all looked after children. Sixty per cent of the looked after children adopted recently in England were aged between one and four. In Scotland, too, this pre-school age group of children formed a significant percentage of children placed for adoption with two – five-year-olds being the largest group. This reflects the wishes of many adopters to parent pre-school children and the relative ease with which adoption agencies are able to recruit adopters for young children. It doesn't reflect the needs of many waiting older children for whom new families are urgently needed.

* Figures are estimated, based on information available from different parts of the UK. There are some variations in the detail of what is collected and the most recent figures available but efforts have been made to ensure that the overall picture is realistic.

** The figures used here exclude those children in Scotland who are "looked after" but who remain at home under supervision from the Children's Hearing system.

The majority of children who wait for adoption are aged five or above. There are single children and groups of brothers and sisters who need placement together and there are children with disabilities who range in age from babies upwards. There are children from a huge variety of ethnic, religious and cultural backgrounds, all of whom need families who match their backgrounds as closely as possible. Many of the children have been abused and/or neglected before they come into local authority care and they will have been further confused and upset by uncertainty and moves after coming into care.

Just as there is a wide range of children needing adoption, so will a wide range of people be welcomed by adoption agencies to adopt them. People of every ethnic, religious and cultural background, couples and single people – heterosexual as well as lesbian and gay, both with or without children – older people, people who have been divorced, all can and do become successful adoptive parents. And the great majority of adoptions work out well. Like all parents, adoptive parents get huge joy and satisfaction from parenting their children, as well as finding it very hard work and sometimes frustrating and painful.

Traditionally, adoption, for children not previously known to the families adopting them, was seen as severing connections with the past and starting afresh. Now we understand how important it is to provide adoptive parents with as much information as possible to pass on to their children, and how important their heritage is for those children. Many adopted children continue to maintain important relationships – sometimes with their birth parents, more often with other family members like brothers and sisters, grandparents, aunts and uncles.

Adoption agencies do not expect you to know all about adoption before you approach them. They will provide information and opportunities for you to find out about what will be involved, for instance, by introducing you to experienced adoptive parents. They are also working hard to provide better help and support to you and your child once you are living together and after you have adopted. Help is also available from adoptive parents' support groups and, in England and Wales, from post-adoption centres.

We hope that this book will answer most of your initial questions as well as clarify anything that may have previously puzzled you about adoption – the processes, the cost, the legal issues, etc. All these and many other issues are addressed in this book. These are illustrated with real life experiences in which people candidly talk about what went right and what went wrong and how they were helped or helped themselves create a safe, secure and loving family environment for a child or children who needed this. For children who have to be separated from their birth families, having a new permanent family by adoption is an experience that must fulfil *their* needs and help them through to a fulfilling adulthood.

A glossary of terms that are used in this book and which may be unfamiliar to you is provided at the end.

Changes in the law

The Adoption and Children Act 2002 was finally fully implemented in England and Wales on 30 December 2005. It is underpinned by more than ten sets of regulations and also by Statutory Guidance. The changes brought about by this significant new Act are detailed in this edition. Practice Guidance on assessing adopters is expected in March 2006.

In Scotland an Adoption Policy Review has just finished the consultation stages and new legislation is anticipated in the middle of 2008.

There are National Minimum Standards for adoption work in England and Wales and National Care Standards for adoption work in Scotland. These standards form the basis for inspection of adoption services.

Your local BAAF office or a local adoption agency will be able to give you up-to-date information and there are links to the Standards and legislation on www.baaf.org.uk.

Adoption is changing and developing and it will be important for you to check with BAAF and/or with a local adoption agency about any significant changes at the time you make your initial enquiries.

Scope of this edition

Almost all the content of this edition applies to England, Wales and Scotland, although recognising that there are variations between the different countries. Most of the text should also be useful in Northern Ireland.

Adoption as a legal process was first established in 1926 in England and Wales and in 1930 in Scotland. Although these are two separate jurisdictions, the legal framework for adoption was very similar and was primarily about legal security for babies relinquished by their birth parents. Now that most children placed for adoption with non-relatives have spent a period looked after by the local authority, planning for them must also take account of other child care legislation. There is wider variation in this between Scotland and England and Wales, especially given the role of the Children's Hearing system in Scotland. Devolution too is playing more of a part. The statutory basis for the service is first of all in the primary legislation and then in the regulations that provide more detail.

There is one Adoption and Children Act for England and Wales but separate regulations. Scotland will continue to have its own legislation and regulations for all aspects of adoption. Northern Ireland tends to look towards England and Wales in developing its legislation.

However, there are some differences in practice and procedures. In Northern Ireland there are still a number of babies who come into or are removed to care at a very early age and proceed to adoption once they have been "freed" for adoption. However, adoption as a route out of care for older children is not widely used, although efforts are being made to develop this.

As stated previously, most of the text that follows will be relevant to any part of the UK but more information about local variations can be obtained from BAAF's regional centres (see Chapter 9). The legislation provides for children moving from one legal jurisdiction to another so that children can be linked with families across the UK.

Just as the law has been updated over the 70-plus years that adoption has been possible, so practice has changed tremendously. The rest of this book will tell you more about this. One aspect of this that affects the delivery of adoption services is the change in local government. At first, much of the adoption service was provided by voluntary adoption agencies. Now there are fewer such agencies and most children placed are the responsibility of their local authority Social Services or Social Work Departments, which also act as adoption agencies to recruit and prepare adopters. A number of the recently established unitary councils have been looking at different ways of delivering services. Social services may now be joined with education or housing services so that where reference is made to Social Services or Social Work Departments or Directors, you may need to check the precise names/designations locally. Although these terms are not accurate when applied to Northern Ireland, as described below, we have used them for the sake of simplicity.

In Northern Ireland, personal social services are provided by 11 Health and Social Services Trusts in turn commissioned by four Health and Social Services Boards. Unlike England and Wales and Scotland, social services are not under local authority control. A list of all agencies appears later on in this book.

1

Children needing adoption

I wanted a family that would take care of
me and not leave me alone. And when I
want them, they always come. And feed
me properly, and look after me, and be
kind...
Girl aged 8, *Adopted Children Speaking*

Probably at least 5,000 children currently in the care system in England, Scotland and Wales could be placed for adoption with families if the families were available. Although the children are very different, they all have one thing in common: a need for a family.

It is recognised that, for nearly all children, life in a family is best. A new family can bring love and security to the child – and a child can bring joy and satisfaction to the family. Every child is different and brings the potential for different sorts of satisfaction just as they will bring their own set of needs and challenges. The agency's job, with your help, is to match that child's potential and needs with your abilities and expectations.

Are there any babies needing adoption?

Of the 3,800 looked after children adopted in England in the year to March 2005, just 210 were babies under one. Proportionate figures for Scotland are similar – probably no more than 20 infants were adopted. Today it is easier for women to choose to parent on their own and fewer single mothers are placing their babies for adoption. Contraception is more efficient than it used to be, and fewer unplanned pregnancies occur. It is also easier to terminate pregnancies than previously.

There are more white people interested in adopting a white baby without disabilities than there are such babies needing adoption. Agencies have no difficulty in finding suitable adopters for white babies without disabilities and many already have quite a few prospective adopters approved and waiting to adopt. This means that people who want to adopt only such a child are likely to find it hard even to get started on the adoption process and most will not be able to adopt a baby.

By contrast, agencies are less successful at finding black families or those from other minority ethnic groups, although they are getting better at it. This means that if you and/or your partner are black or from a minority ethnic group, you are likely to find an agency to take up your application quite quickly. You will probably have a shorter wait before being linked with a baby although this will vary as only quite small numbers of black babies and those from other minority ethnic groups are placed for adoption each year. If you can consider slightly older children, your wait could be shorter.

There are some babies with disabilities or disabling conditions such as Down's Syndrome and cerebral palsy who need to be adopted. There are also some babies with genetic factors in their background, such as schizophrenia or Huntington's Chorea, for whom it is not always easy to find adoptive families.

Toddlers and pre-school children

Children aged between one and five are the largest group of children adopted in the UK. This reflects the wishes of many adopters to parent pre-school children and the relative ease with which adoption agencies are able to recruit adopters for young children. The majority of these placements work out extremely successfully. However, these children often have complex needs. They may have been abused and neglected and given little opportunity to make attachments to reliable parent figures. They may be very confused about all that has happened in their short lives and unable to trust in anyone. In addition, there may also be uncertainties about their development which may not be resolved until they are older. Families need to be able to take on these issues and to access support and advice.

What about older children?

The majority of children waiting to be adopted are aged five or over. They may have lived for some years with one or both of their parents, or other family members, or they may have had many moves in and out of foster homes, and the damage done by these experiences can last a very long time. Older children need especially resilient parents who can help them face up to the past – including their possible need to keep in touch with some members of their family – and see them through the difficult adolescent years to maturity. In a loving and secure home, most of these children will eventually begin to thrive, although the older they are, the longer it may take.

Won't older children have a lot of problems?

Children who have been looked after by a local authority for months or years are likely to have emotional and behavioural problems because of the experiences which led to them having to be separated from their birth families, but also because of not having a permanent parent figure in their lives. Even young children soon learn that there isn't much point in getting attached to an adult who is soon going to disappear out of their lives. They may find it difficult to become attached to a new family and may act up or test out the new parents in an effort to get the attention they have been missing. Young children may be more like babies in their behaviour sometimes, and even teenagers may act like very young children. But most children of all ages can eventually settle down when they realise that they really are part of the family.

There are some children who have been so hurt by their past experiences that they will go on having special needs throughout their childhood, even though they have clearly benefited from becoming a loved member of the family. If you choose to adopt a

> On a bad day I see the damage and wonder how I'll ever give enough, how I'll ever make enough of an impact to compete and triumph over the impact of the abuse that has robbed my daughter of years of her life and has the potential to rob her of her whole life...On a good day I know I am winning and feel I am the luckiest mother in the world.
> Adoptive mother in *Adoption Today*, Spring 2005

child who may have particular ongoing needs, you should ensure
that the agency will make arrangements for them to have any special
help they may continue to require on a long-term basis.

| Groups of brothers and sisters

Over half of all the children waiting for adoptive families are in
groups of brothers and sisters needing to be placed together. Most of
these children are in groups of two or three, although there are some
groups of four or more. Brothers and sisters can provide support and
comfort for each other throughout their lives. If they want to stay
together and if an assessment of their needs has shown that one
family could parent them successfully, it is very sad if they have to be
separated because no families come forward for them all. You may be
daunted by the practicalities, but extra help and support could and
should be available (see Chapter 4). Brothers and sisters share a
family history and can support each other in making sense of what
has happened to them. Research indicates that, compared to children
of the same age placed on their own, brothers and sisters placed
together are probably more likely to have a successful outcome.

| Disabled children

Disabled children may be placed for adoption at a very young age
when their parents feel unable to care for them, or they may be
looked after by the local authority after their parents have tried
unsuccessfully to cope. So they may feel the impact both of their
disability, the loss of their family of origin, and perhaps the
confusion of a residential setting where different staff come and go.

> **Our twin boys joined us when they were
> three...Direct contact is planned with
> their other siblings twice a year. The
> boys don't have memories of living with
> them so we are going into the unknown,
> but so far their relationships seem very
> positive. We talk about their siblings and
> have photos around the home.**
> Adoptive parent in *Be My Parent*

People who adopt these children will need to be prepared for a challenging yet rewarding task, as some of the children will never be able to lead entirely independent lives. In some cases, experience of disability in prospective adopters – either their own personal or professional experience or that of their children – will be positively welcomed (see *Whatever Happened to Adam?* in Useful Reading).

Learning disabilities/difficulties

There are many babies and older children who have learning difficulties/disabilities waiting for adoption, for example, children with Down's Syndrome or foetal alcohol syndrome. These are children who, as well as individual love and care, need additional help and support to enable them to participate in as many as possible of the experiences and opportunities open to any other child.

There are many children whose learning disabilities are not clearcut: they may have suffered an accident or injury while very young which has affected their ability to learn or to understand the world around them – but no one knows how much. Or they may have been born with a disability that isn't clear to doctors. They may have been neglected and/or abused as a baby and young child, and the extent of the damage this has caused and the possibility of change may still be unclear.

Physical disabilities

There are many types of physical disability – cerebral palsy, muscular dystrophy, spina bifida and cystic fibrosis are just some of

> **Our fourth birth child taught us not to be afraid of disability. She was born with Edward's Syndrome, and through this we became aware of the disabled children left in hospital because their parents found it too difficult to cope. So we decided to adopt.**
> Adoptive mother of two disabled children in *Could you be my Parent?*, taken from *Be My Parent* November 2005

them. Children with these disabilities need the love and security that
life in a family offers just as much as other children do. And, like
most children, they will give love and affection in return. Having a
physical disability does not mean having a learning disability too,
although people sometimes confuse the two. People with physical
disabilities can lead increasingly independent lives nowadays –
especially if they have the support of a loving family.

Are both black and white children waiting to be adopted?

Yes, there are children from a great variety of ethnic, cultural and
religious backgrounds waiting for adoption. They all need families
who match their culture, "race", religion and language as closely as
possible.

Do the children all have contact with their birth families?

It depends on what is meant by contact. It can mean anything from
an adoption where the child has regular face-to-face contact with
members of his or her birth family to an adoption where the adopters
have met the birth parents once and there is an annual letter
exchanged via the adoption agency. Many children being placed for
adoption now will have a plan for their adoptive parents to have at
least an annual exchange of news with their birth family via the
adoption agency. Others will need and want to meet members of
their birth family, sometimes grandparents, brothers and sisters, as
well as their parents, perhaps twice a year.

> **I'm from Jamaica and my husband is
> Scottish. We were shocked when we
> learnt how many children with one black
> and one white parent are in the care
> system. We've adopted Jamie, who is
> now four and we've just been matched
> with a little brother for him, who is two.**
> Adoptive mother

Contact must be planned to meet the child's needs. These will change over time and everyone involved needs to be prepared to be flexible. Contact can often be very positive and can result in a child being more rather than less settled in their new family. Contact can sometimes be easier for everyone to manage if, as described above, the child's adopters match their heritage as closely as possible. You will need to be clear what the plan for contact is for any child whom you plan to adopt.

It's quite clear that she loved him and still loves him really and still thinks of him, so I think that's a positive thing. I mean, it's hard for a child to understand, but I think it's good for him to know that. I think that's a real, positive thing that comes out of the letter contact.
Adoptive mother in *Staying Connected*

2

Who can adopt?

A lot of people don't really understand about adoption and fostering. They seem to think that the adopted child is a kind of second-class child that you can't love as much as your own child. Adoption involves a bond that is just as deep as with birth children.

A birth, adoptive and foster mother in *Could you be my Parent?*

Are there long waiting lists for adopters?

No. It is estimated that at least 5,000 children looked after by local authorities in England, Scotland and Wales could be adopted if enough adopters came forward. They are children like those described in the previous chapter and adopters, both couples and single people, those with or without children already and people of various ages are urgently needed to offer them a chance of family life. The only group of children for whom there are more potential adopters than there are children, are white babies and toddlers without disabilities. Rather than keeping waiting lists of people wanting to adopt this group of children, agencies may have their lists closed. They then just recruit a few families as and when they need them for this small group of children.

Do I have to be "special" to adopt?

No, but understanding, energy, commitment, and the ability to face up to challenges and difficulties are all needed to care for an older child or a child with disabilities or a group of brothers and sisters.

Just as you will be providing support and understanding to a child with a variety of different needs, so you will need support yourself. Your family, including your children if you have any, plus your close relatives and friends, need to be in agreement with your plan, because

We really wanted to adopt a young child, but we knew we'd have to be flexible. Our son, Alex, was only five months old when he came to us. His mother suffers from schizophrenia and his father may do as well and so we've accepted that Alex is more at risk than most people of developing a mental illness when he's older. We'll help and support him all we can should he become ill.
Adoptive father

you will almost certainly call on them for help. Your immediate family will, like yourself, be very closely affected. Children who have been hurt by their experiences can hurt others in their search for security. You will need all the help you can get. In return, though, you will get the joy and satisfaction of seeing some of the emotional damage to a child gradually start to heal. The rest of this chapter gives information on issues which you may be concerned or unsure about. The adoption agencies which you contact will also give you written information on their eligibility criteria for prospective adopters.

| Are there age limits?

You have to be at least 21 years old to adopt in law (unless you are a birth parent involved in a joint step-parent adoption, in which case the age is 18).

There is a greater health risk as people age. Agencies have a responsibility to ensure as far as possible that prospective adopters are likely to be fit and active at least until their child is a young adult. Some adopted adults record their feelings of discomfort at being placed as young children with older adoptive parents. Although there is no upper age limit, many agencies would not usually expect there to be more than about a 45-year age gap between the child and their adoptive parents. However, this is not inflexible and depends partly on what the adopters are offering in relation to the needs of waiting children. The average age of adopters in the UK is currently 38.

Birth mothers placing infants for adoption often ask for their child to be placed with parents within average childbearing ages. So, if agencies do take families on for babies for whom there is a huge choice of families, they may choose to work with slightly younger people.

| Do I have to be married?

No. Single people, both men and women, can and do adopt. The Adoption and Children Act 2002, implemented in England and Wales from 30 December 2005, also enables unmarried couples, whether heterosexual, lesbian or gay, to adopt jointly. People who have been divorced can adopt. If you are married or in a partnership, adoption agencies often prefer you to have been together for several years before taking up an adoption application from you.

| Do I have to be British?

No. You are eligible to adopt a child in the UK if your permanent home is in the UK (the legal term is "domicile") or if you have been habitually resident in the UK for at least a year. If you are adopting as a couple only one of you needs to be domiciled or both of you need to be habitually resident. Habitual residence is quite a difficult status to define and you may need to take legal advice on whether you qualify. You will need to be resident in the UK for long enough to be assessed and approved as adopters, to have a child placed with you and to apply for the court order mentioned. This could take at least two years and possibly longer.

Most children needing adoption will already have had a number of moves. They are likely to be insecure and to need as much stability as possible. They may also have some ongoing contact with members of their birth family. For these reasons it may not be appropriate for many children to be placed with adopters who will be moving around a lot or living overseas after the child's adoption. It is important, too, for children to be placed with families who match their culture, "race", religion and language as closely as possible.

| What if I'm British but working abroad for a few years?

Unless you are making arrangements for the adoption of a child already well known to you, you will almost certainly not be able to adopt a child in the UK until you return to live here.

You usually need, for practical purposes, to be living in the UK for at least two years, so that the adoption agency has a chance to work with you and get to know you, and also to match you with a child and to introduce and place the child. This is followed by a period of at least ten weeks, before you can apply for an Adoption Order. It is not until you have an Adoption Order that you will be able to take the child to live abroad with you.

What if I am disabled or in poor health?

Medical conditions or disability will not necessarily rule you out. All prospective adopters have to have a full medical examination done by their GP. The adoption agency employs a doctor who acts as a medical adviser. He or she will want your permission to contact consultants who have treated you. The adoption agency's prime concern is that you will have the health and vigour necessary to meet the needs of your child until he or she is a young adult.

There is evidence that smoking causes health problems for smokers and that passive smoking can damage the health of others, particularly young children. For this reason, many agencies will not usually place pre-school children with people who smoke.

Excessive alcohol consumption also leads to health problems. It may also be associated, for children in care, with violence and physical abuse. Your drinking habits will therefore need to be discussed with you.

There is also evidence that obesity can cause health problems as can anorexia or other eating disorders and so these conditions are carefully considered by the agency.

What if I've got a criminal record?

People with a record of offences against children or who are known to have harmed children cannot be considered by adoption agencies. A criminal record of other offences need not rule you out. However, the nature of the offence and how long ago it was committed will have to be carefully considered. It is important to be open and honest with the adoption agency early on if you have a criminal record. The information will come to light when the police and other checks are done and any attempt at deception by you will be taken very seriously.

What about finances and housing?

You do not have to own your own home or be wealthy. Adoption agencies prefer there to be a spare bedroom available for a child. However, this isn't a legal requirement and an adopted child could share a bedroom with a child already in your family. Your child would obviously need to be happy about this and it would be helpful if you had a contingency plan in case the children really didn't get on with sharing. You may be eligible to receive financial support from the local authority in certain circumstances, such as if the child whom you wish to adopt has special needs and if you could not afford to adopt him or her otherwise. (Adoption support is described in more detail in Chapter 4.)

Does it matter if we're still having treatment for infertility?

You can certainly get written information from adoption agencies and also attend an information session or ask for an individual interview to find out about adoption. However, you will then need to decide whether to continue with infertility treatment or to pursue adoption. Adoption agencies will not usually be prepared to embark on a full adoption assessment and preparation with you while you are still actively involved in infertility treatment. It can be very difficult to pursue two different routes to parenting at the same time. Experience shows that most people need to end treatment and "mourn" the birth child whom they are not going to have before moving on to think positively about all the issues involved in adoption.

We'd like to adopt a child the same age as our son so that they can grow up together

There is quite a lot of research evidence which shows that it is more likely that things will not work if a child joining a family is close in age to a child already there. Agencies, therefore, usually prefer to have an age difference of two years or more between children. It is also often easier for the new child if he or she can join your family as the youngest child. However, it is possible for children to come in as the eldest or as a middle child, so do discuss this with the adoption agency if you feel it might work in your family.

I'm white and I'd like to be considered for black children as well as white children

The Guidance to the Children Act 1989 for England and Wales states that 'it may be taken as a guiding principle of good practice that, other things being equal and in the great majority of cases, placement with a family of similar ethnic origin and religion is most likely to meet a child's needs as fully as possible and to safeguard his or her welfare most effectively'. The Adoption and Children Act 2002 further states that 'In placing the child for adoption, the adoption agency must give due consideration to the child's religious persuasion, racial origin and cultural and linguistic background.'

The Guidance to the Children (Scotland) Act 1995 states that 'When considering the type of placement to be chosen, regard should be paid to a child's racial, religious, cultural and linguistic background. As far as possible, this background should be catered for within the placement, with carers...sharing the child's religion and heritage. If possible, the location of the placement should not isolate the child from his or her community or cause him or her to experience prejudice.'

Doctors told us that there was no chance of us conceiving a second child. Our son, Mark, is now nine and very much wants a younger brother or even a sister! We saw Joshua in *Be My Parent*. He's only six but he's already been excluded from school once. His local authority are assessing us just for him. We're excited although we know he'll be a challenge for us.
Adoptive mother

There are more white children than black children needing adoption and so it makes much more sense for white families to adopt white children whose particular needs they can meet as fully as possible. For instance, agencies would try to place a child from an Irish Catholic background with Irish Catholic adopters rather than with an English family who are Baptists.

We have to accept the fact that racism is still common in Britain today. So black children – including those of mixed (black and white) heritage who will be identified as black – will, sooner or later, have to cope with some form of racism. A black child who faces racist abuse outside the home will find it easier to discuss what has happened, understand it, and learn how to deal with it from a black adopter who can immediately relate to this experience. Coping with racism is something white people are not geared to, whereas for black adults it is a fact of life. Black children need this level of support in their daily life.

Black children also need black adults they can look up to. Images of black people on television, radio and in newspapers are often negative, although this is changing. Black children need to have black adults with whom they can identify positively. For children who have been unable to stay with their own black families and who are then placed in white families, it can be hard to correct the false impression that white is better than black.

For black children and those from other minority ethnic groups, maintaining links with family members is important just as it would be for a white child. Matching heritage between a child and the adoptive family will make it easier for the child to settle, will help facilitate any continuing birth family contact, and will have the long-term advantage of the child learning about his or her heritage and culture.

However, sometimes a black family cannot be found within timescales which meet the needs of the child. In those instances where white families do adopt black children, they will need to ensure that their children can interact with members of their own community; if they live in a predominantly "white" area, the child will not be able to do this and may feel isolated and may be singled out, for example, at school. Families will also need to enable the child to learn about and take pride in their cultural heritage as well as to prepare them for facing racism in the world outside. This subject is tackled in greater detail in the companion book *Talking about Adoption to your Adopted Child* (see Useful Reading).

I'm worried about an open adoption. Will this rule me out?

It depends what you mean by an open adoption. The term is used to mean anything from a one-off meeting with your child's birth parents and an annual exchange of news via the adoption agency to regular face-to-face contact between your child and members of their birth family. It is recognised now that it be helpful for some children to maintain some face-to-face contact, perhaps with a grandparent or a brother or sister placed elsewhere and sometimes with their birth parents. Face-to-face contact is not the plan for all children and you can discuss with the agency your wish not to have a child who needs this to be linked with you.

However, *all* adoptive parents need to have an open attitude to their child's birth family and past. You need to recognise the importance of this for your child and be prepared to talk with your child about his or her often confused feelings about their birth family and their past. You also have to accept that things can change and that your child *may* want direct contact in the future even though that isn't the plan now.

> I wanted him to see that I did want, I do want, his mum to know about him...I want him to know that it's alright. I want him to know that I want his mum to know about him. I want him to know that I do really have compassion for his mum.
> Adoptive mother in *Staying Connected*

A one-off meeting with birth parents can be very valuable in helping you talk with your child about their birth family and it can be reassuring for the child to know that you have met his or her birth parents. Most adoption agencies would expect you to be prepared for a one-off meeting. They would also expect that you could consider at least an annual exchange of news, usually anonymously via the adoption agency, with your child's birth parents.

Can I adopt my foster child?

This is discussed in Chapter 7.

Can I adopt a member of my family?

The law in both England and Wales and in Scotland allows a child to be placed for adoption by a parent with the child's brother, sister, uncle, aunt or grandparent, without this needing to be agreed by an adoption agency.

For a child who is unable to live with his or her birth parents, living with a member of their extended family may well be the next best thing. However, there are other ways to give the child security which may be better than adoption. For instance, a Special Guardianship Order or a Residence Order gives the carers parental responsibility without taking this away from the birth parents and cutting the child off from them legally, as an Adoption Order does. If you are considering adopting a family member, you may find it helpful to talk this through with a social worker from the local authority where you live, before you apply. There is more

> If you are critical of the people who are part of your child's make-up, then you are rejecting part of them. But if you accept and empathise with the past then you can make a good life for your child. The gains are enormous.
> Adoptive mother in *Could you be my Parent?*

information on Special Guardianship and Residence Orders in Chapter 7.

If you decide to go ahead with the adoption you can start the process for applying to court. The Adoption and Children Act 2002 for England and Wales requires that at least three months before applying to a court to adopt you must notify the social services department of the local authority where you live of your intention to apply. The Act also requires that the child must have lived with you for at least three years out of the last five before you apply. However, you can apply to court for permission to make an application sooner. You can apply to your local Magistrates' Family Proceedings Court, County Court or the High Court.

In Scotland you must also notify the Social Work Department of your intention to adopt. You would then petition the Sheriff Court. The child must have lived with you for thirteen weeks before you can get an adoption order.

The local authority must prepare a comprehensive report for the court. This is called an Annex A report in England and Wales and a section 22 report in Scotland and will involve interviews with you, the child and the child's parents, who will need to consent to the adoption. Medical reports and checks will need to done. Should the child's parents decide to withdraw their agreement at this stage, the court can consider dispensing with it, if there is compelling evidence to do so.

If a child in your family is being looked after by the local authority and seems unlikely to return to his or her parents and you would like to consider offering the child a permanent home, you should contact the child's social worker or local authority as soon as possible. They will welcome your interest.

How do I go about adopting a child?

POSED BY MODELS

We were a bit overwhelmed by the numbers of children featured in *Be My Parent*. However, the staff in *Be My Parent* were really helpful and the social worker from our local adoption agency helped us think about the sorts of children we could parent. We're now hoping to adopt two children aged between four and eight.
Adoptive parents

| First steps

It can be helpful to do some reading about adoption as it is today and about the sorts of children needing families before you approach an adoption agency. This book is a good start and other useful books and leaflets are listed at the end.

Many people thinking about adoption also often find it invaluable to speak to experienced adopters. Adoption UK is a self-help group for adoptive and prospective adoptive parents before, during and after adoption. It has local groups throughout England, Scotland, Wales and Northern Ireland which you could join and whose members will be pleased to talk to you (see BAAF and Other Useful Organisations).

| Contacting an agency

This important step is fully covered in Chapter 9, followed by a complete list of adoption agencies in England, Wales, Scotland and Northern Ireland.

Can I respond to children I see featured in a family-finding magazine before I contact a local agency?

Yes, you can. Social workers featuring children in *Be My Parent*, *Adoption Today*, local newspapers and other media are happy to hear from unapproved families. However, their priority is to place their

> I would encourage anyone to adopt, but you need resilience and support to get through the assessment process. The thing I found hardest was when I would contact a social worker to express an interest in a child and not hear anything for three weeks...I found it very hard to be left in limbo over something so important.
>
> Adoptive parent in *Looking after our Own*

child with a suitable family as soon as possible and so they will follow up approved families first. However, if you are within their geographical catchment area they may well decide to take up an application from you. This might be because you are the most suitable (or the only!) family who has responded to their child. It might also be because they think that you are offering a valuable resource to a child, even if they cannot place the child to whom you have responded with you.

The child's social worker might ask an agency local to you to do the assessment on their behalf, if you live at a distance. Alternatively, he or she might suggest that you contact a local agency, as there are other possibilities for the child whom they have featured. As discussed in Chapter 9, you need to think carefully about being assessed by an agency a long way away as it may be difficult for them to offer you adequate help and support once you have a child placed with you.

What will happen after I've contacted an agency?

Agencies work in slightly different ways. However, you will usually be sent written information initially. You may then be invited to an information meeting with other prospective adopters. If you are still interested, a social worker may then visit you at home or invite you to their office for an individual meeting. Guidance to the Adoption and Children Act in England and Wales and Standards in Scotland

> I sat in the car park for ages, trying to pluck up the courage to get out of the car. I don't know what I was scared of. Not being good enough, I suppose. Once I got in it was fine. Everyone was welcoming and they were a very diverse group of people. I had thought it would be all couples, all white, but there was a real mixture.
>
> Adoptive parent in *Looking after our Own*

give timescales for this part of the process. You should expect to receive written information within five working days of your enquiry (seven in Scotland) and to be invited to a follow-up information meeting within two months. In Scotland an initial interview should be offered within four weeks.

Social workers will discuss some of the issues described in the previous chapter with you. They will also tell you about the children for whom they need families and about the adoption process. They must prioritise applications that are more likely to meet the needs of waiting children. If they decide not to proceed, they should discuss the reasons for this with you and they should inform you in writing.

| The adoption process

Adopters

| Contacting agencies and expressing an interest |
| Information meeting(s) |
| Home visit(s) |
| Application |
| Police, health and other checks |
| Training and preparation |
| Assessment – home study |
| Adoption panel recommendation |
| Agency decision |
| Search for a child |

Child

| Statutory looked after child review |
| Adoption plan agreed |
| Adoption panel recommendation |
| Agency decision |
| Family finding |

| Matching meeting and report |
| Adoption panel recommendation |
| Agency decision |
| Placement planning meeting |
| Possible child appreciation day |
| Introductions |
| Placement |
| Review of placement |
| Adoption application |
| Adoption order |

Making the application, checks and references

If you and the agency do decide to proceed you will be asked to complete an application form. You will be asked for permission to carry out checks which the agency is required to make. They have to check with the police and with the local authority where you live. Many agencies will also want your addresses for the last five or ten years so that they can check whether you were known to those local authorities either, in a way which could be relevant to your ability to parent a child. Agencies may also want to check that you are not seriously in debt and that payments on your home are up to date.

Arrangements will be made for you to have a medical with your GP. You will also be asked to give the names of at least three (two in Scotland) personal referees who will be interviewed. Two of these referees must be unrelated to you, but the other could be a family member. Some agencies ask for more than three referees and will also want to meet relatives from each family, if you are adopting as a couple. The unrelated referees should be close friends who know you well, preferably over quite a long period. If you or your current partner have parented children with a previous partner many agencies will want your agreement to try and interview this person too. They may also ask to talk to adult children whom you have parented.

Preparation and training

Adoption agencies are required to provide preparation for adoption for all prospective adopters. Almost all adoption agencies will ask you to attend a series of group meetings, where you can meet other prospective adopters and can learn with them something of what adoption and being an adoptive parent is all about. Adopted adults, experienced adopters and birth parents whose children have been adopted often speak at these meetings. You will be given opportunities to think about the impact of an adopted child on your family and about how you will need to adapt your current lifestyle.

The issues covered will include:

- why children need to be adopted;

- issues of loss, separation and trauma;

- how children become attached to their carers and the effect on them of the poor attachments which they may have experienced;

- the significance of continuity and contact for children who are separated from their birth family;

- the sorts of behaviour which children who have been neglected and abused may display;

- support networks and support services.

What is the assessment or home study?

This is the process by which the adoption agency gets to know you and assesses your ability to parent an adopted child. It is also the process by which you learn about what will be involved in this parenting task and consider, in partnership with the social workers, whether you have the necessary skills and strengths. You will need to be open and honest with the social workers. They need to know what your limitations are (everyone has some) so that they can make sure that suitable help and support are provided and so that they can match a child with you whose needs you can meet. A social worker (or possibly two) will visit you at home probably about six to eight times. They will meet with you individually as well as together, if you are a couple, and will also want to talk to your own children, if you have any. This will also be the social worker who meets and talks with your personal referees.

Some of the issues which will be covered with you will be:

- your personality and interests;

- your experience of being parented and your own parenting experience, if any;

- your life history;

- your relationships, past and present;

- your wider family and support network;

- your ethnicity, culture and religion;

- your reasons for wanting to adopt, including your feelings about involuntary childlessness;

- your openness towards birth families;

- employment, education and finance.

Although this process is thorough and searching many prospective adopters actually quite like the opportunity to reflect on their life and on their relationships and find it a stimulating and interesting experience. Often, a good and trusting relationship is built up with the social worker.

What exactly are they looking for?

Social workers are looking for people who are open and honest about their limitations as well as their strengths; people who are adaptable and flexible and willing to learn; people who enjoy children and are willing and able to put the child's needs first; people who know that

> The assessment process was very intrusive...I was being asked questions that I am not sure I had even asked myself...If I thought any question was unreasonable, I asked why she wanted to know and she was always able to explain why the information was needed...It was really important that it gave as accurate a picture of me as possible, since it was going to be used to make decisions about what sort of child would be right for me and vice versa.
> Adoptive parent in *Looking after our Own*

every child, even a tiny baby, comes with a past and a birth family who are important; and people with "staying power" and a sense of humour.

What can I do if I have concerns at this stage?

If you are concerned that adoption, at this stage in your life, may not be right for you, you should discuss this with your social worker. You can, of course, withdraw from the process at any point. It is much better to be open about any doubts or concerns that you have at this stage rather than waiting until you are linked with a child.

You may still be keen on adoption but, as happens occasionally, be finding it difficult to work with your social worker. You need to try to share your concerns with your worker but if you can't resolve things between you, you could consider contacting their manager for help. It is possible, although quite unusual, to have a change of worker part-way through the process.

You can, of course, withdraw your application from that agency at any point. However, if you apply elsewhere you may well have to start again from the beginning. The second agency will also need to contact the first one for any comments which they may have. You should be able to see anything which is put in writing (provided it doesn't include third party information, for example, from your referees).

The assessment report

A written report will be compiled, with your help. BAAF's Form F1 is the form most often used to collate this information. You must be given a copy of the report to read, apart from the medical information, checks and information from your personal referees (which remain confidential to the agency). You have ten working days (under English regulations) in which to comment, in writing if necessary, on anything that you disagree with the social worker about or that you think should be added.

| The adoption panel

The report is presented to the agency's adoption panel for their recommendation. This is a group of about ten people, including social work professionals, a medical adviser, a councillor (although a councillor is not required in Scotland) and independent members, who are people with knowledge of and an interest in adoption. These almost always include at least one adoptive parent and an adopted adult. The regulations about membership of panels are different in England and Wales from Scotland, but their purpose is the same: to consider prospective adopters and to make a recommendation to the agency about whether they are suitable to adopt or not.

You must be invited to attend the panel, or at least part of it, if you wish. Most prospective adopters do attend. Most are very nervous beforehand but find the actual experience less daunting than they thought. Panel members find it extremely helpful to meet prospective adopters and to have the opportunity to have a brief discussion with them.

The panel may consider and give advice to the agency about the number, age range, sex, likely needs and background of children whom you could adopt. However, it is the agency which makes the final decision on this.

| The final decision

After the panel has made its recommendation, a senior officer in the agency considers whether or not to approve you as an adopter. In England and Wales, if the agency is proposing not to approve you, they must write to you first giving you their reasons and asking for your comments. In England, applicants at this stage have 40 days within which to make comments (representations), either to the decision maker or to the Independent Review Mechanism (IRM) (see below), but not to both. In England, Wales and Scotland, the agency must write and tell you their final decision, whether it is approval or non-approval. It should be unlikely for you to get to this stage and not be aware of any concerns about you from your social worker. Research indicates that 94 per cent of people who get to this stage in the process are approved as adopters.

| A brief report

Occasionally social workers will decide, before they have completed the assessment, that they will not be able to recommend you as suitable to adopt. They will discuss their concerns with you and you will have the option of withdrawing from the process. However, if you decide that you want to proceed, the social workers can write a brief report which, in England, is then treated in the same way as a full report, i.e. you must see it and can comment on it, it will go to the panel and then to the decision maker. If the decision maker proposes not to approve you, you will have the right to apply to the IRM (provided that your agency is in England).

| IRM

This is run by BAAF under contract to the Department for Education and Skills. It is only available to people assessed by adoption agencies in England. If you receive written notification from the agency, following a panel, that it proposes not to approve you (or to terminate your approval), you can apply to the IRM. You must do this within 40 days. The IRM will arrange for your case to be heard by an independent IRM panel, which you can attend. The IRM panel will make a recommendation which will go to your agency. The agency decision maker will then make the final decision.

An Independent Review Panel process will also operate for people assessed by agencies in Wales. It is run by the Welsh assembly.

| What happens if I'm not approved?

If the agency has not been able to approve you, you should discuss with them fully the reasons why. They will have been disappointed not to be able to approve you and will have thought about this very carefully and so you may agree with them that perhaps adoption is not for you. In Scotland, guidance states that 'agencies may find it helpful to establish a reconsideration procedure for adoptive applicants' and a number of agencies in Scotland do this. However, you can, if you wish, approach other adoption agencies and start again. Sometimes, people turned down by one agency are approved by another and go on to adopt successfully.

If you feel that the service that you have had from the agency has been poor you can, if you wish, make a formal complaint about this to the agency.

How long will it all take?

This process, from your formal application to approval by the agency, should not usually take more than eight months. This is the timescale in the Guidance to the Adoption and Children Act for England. National Care Standards for Scotland suggest a similar timescale of around seven months. The whole process is described more fully in BAAF's leaflet, *Understanding the Assessment Process* (see Useful Reading).

Do I have to pay the agency?

There is no charge for the home study, assessment and preparation if you are adopting a child who is in the UK. However, if you are asking an agency to do a home study so you can adopt a child from abroad, they will probably make a charge (see Chapter 6).

What happens after approval?

If you have been approved by a local authority, they will consider you carefully for their waiting children. They will usually want you to wait for one of their children, or for a child from the local consortium of agencies to which they may belong, for three months, before responding to children featured in family-finding magazines by other agencies. You may want to check on this before deciding to work with them. If you are still waiting after this agreed period of up to three months, the local authority should, with your agreement, refer you to the Adoption Register for England and Wales for active consideration for children referred to the Register.

If you have been approved by a voluntary adoption agency, they will help you to find a waiting child. They will encourage you to respond to children in *Be My Parent*, *Adoption Today* and other media, and they will probably agree to refer you to the Adoption Register straightaway.

It is only adoption agencies in England and Wales which can refer adopters and children to the Register. (See Useful Organisations for more information on the Register.)

Considering possible children

Your agency may approach you to discuss a possible child or you may respond to a child whom you see featured as needing a new family. You will probably talk with your own social worker first and will then meet the child's social worker and also, perhaps, their foster carer. You will also be given written information about the child. It is important, in the excitement of hearing about a possible child at last, that you take time to consider the child's needs carefully and how you will be able to meet them. You may want to follow up particular issues with the social workers or the foster carers or with a doctor, or check whether the necessary services, for example, special schooling, are available in your area. It is important that you have as much information as possible about the

Be assertive and don't let things drift. The adoption process is slow and seems to take forever. But you can help to move some things along more quickly. For instance, if people don't return your calls, ring them again...and again...and again!
Adoptive parent in *Could you be my Parent?*

child and their background. Your social worker has a responsibility to ensure that you receive this and should help you consider it.

The child's social workers may still be considering other families at this stage. They should keep you and your social worker in touch with what is happening. If they decide that another family has more to offer this particular child they should try to explain this to you.

Being matched with a child

The Adoption Agencies Regulations for England introduce fairly detailed requirements for this part of the process. Arrangements in other parts of the UK will be broadly similar but not identical.

Once the child's social workers have decided that you seem to be the right family for a particular child and you are also keen to proceed, they must give you a copy of the child's permanence report (a comprehensive report about the child, comparable to your Form F1). They must also give you any other reports and information on the child's health, education or special needs which would be helpful. They should meet with you to discuss all this, including the plans for any post-placement contact for the child with birth relatives or others. If you and they are keen to proceed, they should then assess what adoption support you and the child will need.

The social workers should then write an adoption placement report which should include the proposed contact and support arrangements. You must be given 10 days to read and comment on this.

> **What did I want to know about my new family? Everything! What were they like? How old were they? What were their hobbies? What did they like doing? What didn't they like doing? What kind of children they'd like, boy or girl? Everything.**
> Girl in *Adopted Children Speaking*

This report plus your Form F1 and the child's permanence report will be presented to an adoption panel, usually the one in the child's local authority. Your social worker and the child's social worker will attend and many agencies will also invite you to attend. It can be extremely helpful to the panel if you can do so.

As with your approval as an adopter, it is a senior officer who makes the decision about the match, based on the recommendation of the panel.

What support and help will be available?

It is very important that you discuss with both the child's social worker and with your social worker at this matching stage, what sort of support and help you and the child will need after placement. As described above, there should be a written plan, discussed and agreed with you, about this. It should cover any special arrangements which need to be made to meet the child's educational and health needs and any therapy which may be needed. It should also cover the support and help which will be available to you. If you will need financial help, the necessary means test should be done and an agreement made as to the level and frequency of any payments.

One adoptive parent, if in employment, is now entitled to statutory adoption leave for one year. This is currently paid at the lower of £106 or 90 per cent of average weekly earnings, for the first six months. The other parent, if there are two, if employed, is entitled to

> I think you're so nervous about meeting the people because you know they've chosen you because they think you're better. I mean they've looked through a whole catalogue or magazine...and seen you and thought that's who they wanted. So you feel nervous about meeting them. You think, 'Well, am I going to be good enough?'
> Girl in *Adopted Children Speaking*

two weeks' statutory leave at the same rate. To qualify for either, you must have completed 26 weeks continuous service with your employer up to the date of matching.

What is a child appreciation day?

Some, but not all, agencies arrange these days. They invite all the key people who have known the child, such as former foster carers, teachers and relatives, to meet with you. This enables you to build up a really detailed and "living" picture of the child and their life so far.

How long will it be before my child comes to live with me?

Once a decision has been made about a match, the social workers will meet with you to confirm plans for support, for contact with the birth family, for your exercise of your parental responsibility and for introductions. They will work out with you and with the child's foster carers a plan for introducing you and the child to each other. Introductions may be daily for a week for a young baby, or rather more spaced out over a longer period for an older child. They do not usually last more than six to eight weeks though.

You should discuss any doubts or concerns that you may have with the social workers during this period. If you really do not feel that the match is right it is much better to say so at this stage rather than later.

> The introduction period was extremely tiring both mentally and physically, so we were glad when Luke moved in. He was very excited, but there were moments of sadness too when he missed his previous carers. Once he knew that this was OK, he could talk about them, he started to settle.
> Adoptive mother in *Could you be my Parent?*

What happens after a child moves in?

POSED BY MODELS

At the moment things are fine, but there have been times, and there will be other times, when we need help. So much happened to him in the first three years of his life, and I want to help him, but I don't always know how to deal with his pain. He gets very angry and very sad.

Adoptive parent in *Looking after our Own*

Your child or children moving in is only the beginning. Adjusting to a different way of life will take time and there will be difficult periods. You and your child may well need help and efforts are being made to ensure that this is available.

| Parental responsibility

The Adoption and Children Act 2002 gives adoptive parents in England and Wales parental responsibility on placement, rather than just on adoption, as formerly. You will share this with the child's birth parents and with the local authority which is placing the child with you. The local authority must discuss with you, before they place the child, whether they propose to restrict your exercise of your parental responsibility in any way. You could agree, for instance, that they will still be involved in decisions about visits abroad or health treatment. Once the child is adopted you have exclusive parental responsibility with no restrictions.

| What help will be available?

It is important, as described in the previous chapter, to talk to your social worker and to the social worker for your child, before the child moves in, about the help and support and special services which may be necessary. You should, if you are adopting in England, have a written Adoption Placement Plan, which has been discussed and agreed with you. This should cover support arrangements as well as arrangements for contact with the birth family, and for the exercise of your parental responsibility. If appropriate, referrals should already have been made for specialist therapy or educational or health services which your child may need. This will be especially important if you are adopting an older child who may have experienced considerable trauma, or a child who has suffered from neglect or abuse. In such cases, access to appropriate help will be crucial.

Social workers from the adoption agency which assessed and approved you, as well as from the child's agency, if different, will offer you all the help they can during the settling-in period. They are required to visit at regular intervals and to review how things are going. Adoption UK also offers invaluable support and help to adoptive families, and there are local groups throughout the UK.

Will there be any financial help?

You should be clear before the child moves in about any practical and financial support which can be given. Many local authorities pay a settling-in grant, especially if you are adopting older children, which could be several hundred pounds, to cover your initial outlay on equipment such as beds and car seats. If you are adopting a group of brothers and sisters, it is possible for them to pay towards, for example, a larger car and for equipment such as a large washing machine. Regular financial support may be available for certain children, a group of brothers and sisters, for example, or a child with disabilities or with serious behaviour difficulties. This regular financial support is means tested but you should enquire about this if you think you need this help at any stage. There is an annual paper review of your means, which determines the level of the financial support.

Will support be available after adoption?

Many adoption agencies now have "after adoption" or "post-adoption" workers. They keep in touch and offer the opportunity to

> There was a part of me where I just wanted...nothing to do with anybody. I did feel like that and that's quite selfish. I was aware that it was selfish and you have to come to terms with it. You can't do that. I had no right to do that to him. He's got other people in his life. It's like me cutting off [my wife] from anybody else – that would be wrong so have to come to terms with it.
> Adoptive father in *Supporting Adoption*

talk over issues. They also often organise group events on subjects such as managing difficult behaviour or talking to children about adoption. They can also help you access specialist services which you and your child may need. Much of the UK (although not Scotland) is also served by After Adoption or Post-Adoption Centres, which exist to help families at this stage. Adoption UK can also provide valuable support from other experienced adopters. Efforts are currently being made to try and improve services around the UK for adoptive families.

Adoption Support Services Regulations for England make it clear that adoptive families have the right to request and be given an assessment of their adoption support needs, including the need for financial help, at any stage in the child's childhood. The responsibility for this assessment stays with the local authority which placed the child for three years after the adoption order. After this, the responsibility for the assessment moves to the local authority in which you live.

What about the birth family?

Birth parents whose children are adopted usually find this a hard and painful experience. Sometimes they have requested adoption, but often the decision has been made by others, sometimes very much against their own wishes. However, they are often still very

> We have annual letterbox contact with our son's birth mother. It's hard work building up to it – I wonder each time what to say, how his birth mother will picture him from the letter and photos...It tears me to shreds, writing a letter once a year. There's a huge sense of relief afterwards. But at the same time I feel overwhelming love for him. It doesn't upset me to send the letter, but brings me that feeling of love.
> Adoptive mother in *Could you be my Parent?*

important to their children and many of them are prepared to co-operate with the adopters and the agency in offering what they can to their child.

It is usually to the benefit of the child if the adopters can meet the birth parents at least once and continue to exchange basic information about the child. This is usually through the adoption agency which acts as a "letter box" for a letter perhaps once a year. It is now recognised that maintaining some level of contact can be of benefit to children as they grow up and helps the adopters answer questions about the birth parents, what they were like, where they are now, and so on. Ongoing contact will not be right in all cases and will need to be handled sensitively.

This is something you and your agency will be discussing right from the start, so that when you become an adoptive parent you will have a clear idea of what sort of contact is likely to be the most helpful for your child. When agencies talk about contact they do not necessarily mean face-to-face meetings – in fact, many arrangements for contact involve keeping in touch through letters and are often through an intermediary such as the agency. Only some contact arrangements, at present, involve regular meetings or phone calls between the child and people from his or her past.

For some children visits may continue after adoption. This may be with birth parents or with grandparents and other significant adults or it may be with brothers and sisters who are living elsewhere, perhaps in other adoptive families. Older children may know where their relatives are living and want a family who can help them keep in contact. Again, this is something that you, the agency, and the child, if old enough, will need to discuss and agree on well before the adoption goes through to court. However, it is important to remember that the child's needs and wishes will change over time and you do need to be prepared to be flexible.

Why do children have to know they are adopted?

Many children who are adopted were old enough when placed to remember something of their past and so they obviously know about their adoption. However, all children have the right to know about their past. Increasingly, it has been acknowledged that an open rather than a secretive attitude is more helpful to the child. After all, there is always the danger that someone else will tell the child without any warning, or perhaps in a hostile way, for example, in a family row. Finding out like this can be a terrible shock to a child who may well wonder what else you have concealed from them.

Even older children may be very confused about what happened in the past. They may blame themselves for the things that went wrong in their birth family. So it is important to be honest and to discuss adoption quite naturally, right from the start.

From the age of 18 in England and Wales and 16 in Scotland, adopted children have the right to their original birth certificate if they want it – although their adoptive parents may already have given it to them.

Adoption means that the new parents must be prepared to be open with their child. The BAAF book, *Talking about Adoption to your Adopted Child*, can help you with the kind of issues you will face (see Useful Reading). This is when the information collected by the adoption agency about the child's birth parents and early life, often in a life story book, will be needed. Children who are not given any

> But of course all isn't perfect. He does push us a lot, he is very stubborn, determined and independent – very strong-minded. He was always very affectionate but sometimes it felt superficial, not deep. It still feels like that sometimes.
> Adoptive parent in *Looking after our Own*

facts sometimes have fantasies about their circumstances or history and may well believe the worst, so it is kinder and fairer to tell them the truth. This is not something that you do just once. Children need to go over their story again at different stages in their growing up, understanding a bit more each time.

What if adoption goes wrong?

Some adoptions do go wrong – like marriages, they do not always work. The first few weeks and months can produce problems that no one anticipated so there is always a settling-in period of at least three months and usually considerably longer, before an Adoption Order is made. Of course, the social worker from the agency will keep in touch with you and will help and support you as much as possible. If you feel that things really are going wrong during this period, and that you cannot continue with the child, you owe it to yourself and to the child to tell the agency.

Once the adoption has been made legal, the child will be legally yours just as if you had given birth to him or her. The sources of help described above will be available. If the problems cannot be resolved, the Social Services or Social Work Department can take responsibility for the child again. However, the adoptive parents will remain the child's legal parents until and unless the child is adopted again by new parents.

What will happen to the child if things don't work out?

If the child does have to leave, he or she will go either to a foster family or possibly to a residential home. If it isn't possible to resolve the difficulties with you, another adoptive home may be found, but the difficulties that arose between you and the child will have to be understood to try and prevent the same thing happening again. Sometimes agencies arrange a meeting, called a disruption meeting, which enables everyone concerned to come together and reflect on events and what can be learned from them. Sometimes the problems arise when the child is much older, 16 plus, and like many teenagers, is having difficulty feeling at home in a family setting. The best solution then may be to support the child in an "independent" setting such as lodgings. He or she may well value having you around to advise and reassure him or her even if living together is too difficult at that point in their lives.

Could I try again?

You may feel you and the child were not right for one another, and that you could succeed with a different child. If the social worker agrees with you, you may get the chance to adopt again. After all, different children need different families and just as a second attempt may work for a child, so it may work for a family. You could apply to the same agency again or to a different one. You would need a further period of assessment and preparation and the adoption panel and the agency would need to consider whether or not to approve you again to adopt.

5

How is adoption made legal?

POSED BY MODELS

I love reading the ending of a book because of the feeling of triumph that you've finished it...and I guess that was the same feeling in court, watching them close the book, really shutting it...Knowing that nothing else was going to happen. It was just going to be an ordinary life from now on.
Girl in *Adopted Children Speaking*

When you adopt a child, you become the child's legal parent. The child usually takes your surname and can inherit from you just as if he or she was born to you. All responsibility for making decisions about the child and his or her future is transferred to the adopters. An adoption is not legal without an Adoption Order made by a court. Once an Order has been made it is irrevocable and cannot be overturned.

How do I get an Adoption Order?

You have to apply to court for an Adoption Order. You apply in England and Wales to your local Magistrates' Family Proceedings Court, to a County Court which deals with adoption (now a network of designated adoption centres), or to the High Court; in Scotland you lodge a petition in the Sheriff Court or the Court of Session; in Northern Ireland you apply to the County Court or to the High Court. Your adoption agency should be able to help you with the process and the court. You will need to obtain an application form from the court and complete and return it. If you are not adopting a child who is looked after by a local authority, you will also need to notify the Social Services or Social Work Department in your area of your intention to adopt at least three months before you apply to court. They will have a duty to visit you and your child and to prepare a report for the court.

When can I apply to court?

The Adoption and Children Act for England and Wales requires that if your child has been placed with you by an adoption agency, he or she must have lived with you in the 10 weeks before you make the application to court. If your child is older or has special needs, you will probably want to wait longer and give yourselves a chance to settle down together properly before applying to court. You will need to discuss with your social worker when the right time would be to apply to court. There are different timescales for relatives, step-parents and others adopting a child who has not been looked

after and placed by an adoption agency. These are detailed in the
relevant chapters. In Scotland, the child must have lived with you
for at least 13 weeks before an adoption order can be made, if placed
by an adoption agency, or 12 months in other cases.

What happens before the court hearing?

Before the court can consider your application, it will require a
social worker from the local authority which placed your child with
you, or from the one where you live if your child was not placed by
a local authority, to prepare a report. This is called an Annex A
report in England and Wales and a section 22 or section 23 report in
Scotland. It is a detailed report which includes information about
your child and their birth family, about you and about the placement,
both the reasons for it and also how it is going. In Scotland, an
independent person appointed by the court called a curator *ad litem*
will prepare a report. In England and Wales a Children's Guardian
(formerly called a guardian *ad litem*) may be asked by the court to
prepare a report in some cases. These workers will need to talk with
you and your child, as well as with the birth parents.

What happens in court?

Adoption hearings are usually very short if the child's birth parents
are in agreement, and in Scotland you may not need to go to court.
You need not expect it to last more than half an hour, and you should
be told at once whether the Adoption Order is granted. A report will
have been prepared for the court which the Judge, Magistrates or
Sheriff will consider. You will probably be asked some questions,
and so will the child, if he or she is old enough. The Judge must
consider the views of the child, taking account of the child's age and
understanding. Also, in Scotland, any child of 12 or over is asked
formally if he or she consents to the adoption. The only reason to
dispense or do away with the child's consent is if he or she is
incapable of consenting.

What if the birth parents don't agree?

In England and Wales, a local authority must have authorisation to place a child with you before it can do so. This authorisation is either formal, signed consent by the child's birth parent(s) or it is a court order, called a Placement Order or a Freeing Order. (Freeing Orders can no longer be applied for since 30 December 2005, but existing ones remain in force.) Once this authorisation has been given and the child has been placed with you and you have applied to court, it will only be in exceptional cases that the birth parents will be able to contest the adoption and they will need the leave of the court to do this.

In Scotland, and in non-agency placements in England and Wales, if the birth parents do not agree, the adopters have to ask the court to override their wishes. The court can only do this in appropriate circumstances, for instance, if it judges that the parents are unreasonably refusing to agree. Cases like this are known as contested adoptions and if you are involved in one you will almost certainly need legal help. You should be able to obtain help with the costs, either through public funding (formerly legal aid) or from the adoption agency, and it is worth finding out about this at an early stage.

What is a freeing order?

Before the Adoption and Children Act 2002 was implemented on 30 December 2005, adoption agencies in England and Wales could apply to court for a Freeing Order for a child, either because the birth parents wanted to agree to adoption early, or because the agency wanted a court to deal with the issue of their consent early in the process. Freeing orders can no longer be applied for but existing freeing orders remain in force. In Scotland, when an adoption agency has decided that adoption is in the best interests of a child, and has notified the birth parents of this, a freeing application will usually have to be made if the birth parents do not agree with the plan. Once the child has been "freed", the birth parents cannot stop an adoption going through.

Are there any other legal issues?

Yes, a few, but if, as is likely, you are adopting through an adoption agency, it will usually sort things out for you. You can only receive a child for adoption in this country if he or she is placed by a UK adoption agency or via the High Court, unless the child is a close relative. Remember that any other private arrangement to adopt is *illegal*.

Will my child get a new "birth certificate" when he or she is adopted?

Yes, your child will be issued with a new short certificate in your name which looks the same as other short birth certificates. If you wish, you can apply for a long "birth" certificate, which will give your names and your child's new name. It will have "Copy of an entry in the adoption register" printed on it.

Isn't going to court expensive?

There is a court fee which is currently £140 in the County Court and the Magistrates' Court in England and Wales. In Scotland the fee at the Sheriff Court is £50. The local authority responsible for the child may be able to help you with part or all of this fee.

> **Our boys were ten and eight when they came to live with us. We couldn't manage without regular financial support, which is paid by the local authority that had looked after the children.**
> Adoptive parents

| **What about legal fees?**

If the birth parents do not agree to the adoption and decide to oppose it in court, it may get so complicated that you need a solicitor and a barrister if in England and Wales, or an advocate in Scotland. This means legal costs can rise, in some cases, to several thousand pounds. But you may be able to claim public funding – it depends on your income – or the local authority responsible for the child will usually pay most, or all, of the legal costs involved.

6

What about adoption from abroad?

POSED BY MODELS

> We would have preferred to have
> applied in the UK but we were told that
> it would be impossible to adopt a baby.
> We decided to try and adopt from India.
> We are both Indian and we still have a
> lot of family there.
> Adoptive parent

Some families are moved by the plight of children who have been the victims of war or natural disaster, or who have been abandoned in orphanages, and come forward to offer a home to such children. Others who may not be able to adopt in the UK the child whom they feel able or want to parent, may also seek to adopt from another country. In some cases, families may want to adopt a child who is a relative and lives in another country.

Where can I get advice and help before deciding on this?

You can approach your local Social Services or Social Work Department. There is also a helpline run by the Department for Education and Skills and another run independently by the Intercountry Adoption Centre. Adoption UK will be able to talk to you about adoption generally and AFAA (Association of Families who have Adopted from Abroad) will be able to help you with some of the issues particular to adoption from abroad. Written information is available from all these agencies and from BAAF (see BAAF and Other Useful Organisations and Useful Reading). Many of the issues that you will need to consider are also relevant to adoption in the UK and are covered in Chapter 2.

Surely adoption overseas is the best plan for children living in large institutions?

It may be the best plan for some children in the short term. However, children have the right to remain in their own family, their own community and their own country, if at all possible, and countries overseas are working to this end. They need help from more affluent countries, and from individuals in those countries, to achieve this. In some countries, the "loss" of their children to overseas adoption has triggered the development of adoption services, and programmes to improve child care services have been launched, sometimes in collaboration with or funded by child care services from more "developed" countries.

As children grow up they may feel anger and sadness and a sense of loss at having been "rejected" not just by their birth family, but by their country of birth. It may be extremely difficult for them to establish any links with their birth family and with their past unless their adoptive parents have made great efforts to keep this alive for them.

If the child has been placed with adoptive parents of a different culture, "race", religion and language, they will also be disadvantaged in establishing a positive sense of identity and cultural heritage, and in coping with any racism which they will encounter. Special efforts will need to be made to help counter this.

Wouldn't countries in crisis welcome this sort of help?

In an emergency, it is impossible to gather the information needed to make a decision about whether the child really needs adoption. For example, are the child's parents alive or not? They may be in hospital, in prison, in hiding or refugees in another country, and may re-emerge to claim their child later. Intercountry adoption is not a suitable way of dealing with the needs of children who are moved as a result of war, famine, or other emergency. Indeed, many of these children will be emotionally damaged by abandonment, malnutrition, the effects of war, and separation from their families. In a crisis, the child needs to be made safe in as familiar an environment as possible. Experienced aid workers find that the vast majority of children separated from their families by war or other emergency can be reunited with relatives when the crisis recedes.

> **We adopted two children from El Salvador. Our son, Luis, isn't interested in his birth family, but our daughter, Alicia, is sad and angry that we have virtually no information about her first family. She blames us for this.**
> Adoptive parent

What is required is temporary care in a secure and loving environment, not the permanence of adoption.

I really only want a child without health problems

There can be no guarantee about this when you adopt from abroad. There is often very little information available about the child's early experiences and medical history or that of their birth parents, all of which will have implications for the child. Depending on the country of origin the child may have been exposed to the risk of conditions such as tuberculosis, HIV infection, hepatitis B and C. Reliable and safe testing may not always be available. The child may also have suffered considerable physical, emotional and intellectual deprivation which may have long-term effects. Other factors, for example, the likelihood of any inherited conditions, will probably never be known until they manifest themselves.

What is the process for adopting from overseas?

You must have a home study done by the Social Services or Social Work Department for the area where you live or by an approved voluntary adoption agency which is also approved as an intercountry adoption agency. It is *illegal* to commission a private home study report. Many of the issues which will be covered in the home study are the same as those discussed in Chapter 3. The assessment process is similar, including the involvement of the

> **Our daughter, Amy, has a serious congenital hearing loss which we didn't know about when we adopted her from China. We love her and we are coping, although we'd always said that we didn't want to adopt a child with a disability.**
> Adoptive parent

adoption panel. If your adoption agency is in England you will also have the option of applying, if necessary, to the IRM.

When the adoption agency has approved you as suitable to adopt from your chosen country the home study report is sent to the Department for Education and Skills (DfES), the Scottish Executive, the National Assembly for Wales or the Northern Ireland Department of Health and Social Services depending, of course, on where you live.* It is they who will then endorse the application.

Is the whole process expensive?

Yes, it certainly can be. Most local authorities in the UK, whose first priority must be the placement of children whom they are already looking after, make a charge for the home study to cover their costs. Charges can be £4,000 or more. There will also be the cost of travel at least once, or possibly more often, to the child's country. Documents need to be translated, there are usually lawyer's fees and there may also be charges made by the agency overseas.

How do I decide which country to apply to?

The home study must be in relation to one country only and it is for you to decide which one. It is likely to be helpful if this is a country with which you already have links or can make links. It will be important for your child that you have knowledge and understanding of the culture, religion and history of the country and, if possible and realistic, some knowledge of the language. You will need to know, or be prepared to get to know, adults from the country who are willing to play a part in your child's life. It can also be helpful to have contact with other families who have adopted children from that country.

---

* In the rest of this chapter Department for Education and Skills (DfES) should be read as including the other equivalent bodies.

How will I be linked with a child?

The process described here is that for England and Wales. You should enquire locally about the slightly different process in Scotland or Northern Ireland. Once the adoption agency has decided on your suitability to adopt and the Department for Education and Skills has endorsed the application, the latter will send all your papers to an agency in the country you have chosen. The authorities in the child's country of residence will decide whether to accept your application, and having done so, your name(s) will be placed on their waiting list for a child. It is the responsibility of the authorities in the child's country of residence to match a child with you.

When the authorities overseas have identified a child for you, they will send you (possibly via the DfES) some information about the child including some medical details. The amount of information provided varies greatly.

When you have received this information, it will be important to discuss it with your own GP and you must also discuss it with your social worker. The agency medical adviser may also be able to give you advice. BAAF's leaflet, *Children Adopted from Abroad: Key health and developmental issues*, will also be useful.

When you have made the decision to go ahead with the proposed match, you will need to make arrangements to travel to the child's country to meet the child. If you are then happy to proceed with the adoption, you must notify your adoption agency of this in writing.

How do I have the child placed with me and bring him or her back to the UK?

The arrangements for this will vary according to the adoption laws and procedures of your chosen country, whether the country has ratified or acceded to the Hague Convention and whether or not it is on the UK's list of designated countries. You will need to comply with the requirements of the child's country as well as with UK immigration requirements. Your adoption agency and the other sources of information already described will be able to advise you.

Will I have to adopt the child again in the UK?

As described above, this will depend on the country which your child comes from and the arrangements made for the placement in that country. It will be necessary in some situations to apply to adopt to a UK court once you have returned here with the child.

What support will be available after I adopt?

The adoption agency which does your home study should discuss with you what support they can offer after adoption. There are post-adoption centres in England and Wales which can help you and there are also two main support groups of adoptive parents, Adoption UK and AFAA (see BAAF and Other Useful Organisations). There are also groups of adopters who have adopted children from particular countries. Adoption UK, AFAA or the Intercountry Adoption Centre should be able to give you information on these.

I would like to adopt a child overseas who is related to me

If there has been a crisis in your extended family overseas and, for instance, a child's parents have died suddenly, you can apply for that child to join you in the UK as a dependant. You need to apply to the nearest British diplomatic post in the child's country. If it is agreed that the child has no other family locally able or willing to care and that the child needs to join you, entry clearance to the UK and indefinite leave to stay may be granted. Once the child has settled with you in the UK, you can decide whether or not adoption would be a good idea.

However, it may be that a relative overseas is planning to help you in your wish to be a parent by giving you one of their children, or you may wish to adopt a child in your extended family overseas who is living in poverty or difficult circumstances. The process in this situation would be to apply to an adoption agency here for a home study, as described earlier in this chapter, but to check out at the same time, through the British diplomatic post in the child's country and the Immigration Department of the Home Office here, whether entry clearance would be likely to be granted. It is unlikely that it would be granted for a child who is being "gifted" to you. Adoption has to be about meeting the needs of a child who is unable to live with their birth parents or other local relatives and who needs to be adopted.

What about fostering?

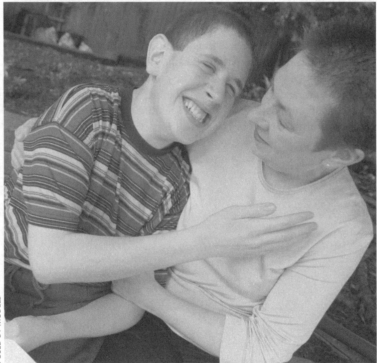

There are kids who fit really well into
your family and are easy to care for.
Then there's kids you want to like but
can't help but think, when is this kid
leaving us? Still, you do your best for all
of them, 'cause that's what you're doing
it for, and you want to do a good job
every time.
Ruth, foster carer

Fostering is a way of providing family life for someone else's child in your home. Most of the children looked after by local authorities when their own families are unable to care for them are placed in foster families. There are roughly 53,000 children in foster care in the UK, 65 per cent of all looked after children. Families are unable to care for their children for a variety of reasons. Sometimes parents have poor physical or mental health and have to be hospitalised, or they may abuse drugs or alcohol and need help to overcome their addiction. Children may have been neglected and they may also have been abused.

What about the foster child's parents?

Fostering is shared caring. Foster carers are not the child's legal parents and do not have parental responsibility. They usually share the caring with the child's birth parents, as well as with the local authority. Being a parent whose child is in foster care is painful, and foster carers need to understand this and be sympathetic. Although they are not living with them, their parents are still very important to children who are fostered. Usually, they will want to see them often and parents will have a big part to play in making plans for the children's future, so foster carers and parents generally work closely together to do what is best for the children. Seventy per cent of children who are looked after return home within a year.

Children in foster care are often visited by their parents in the foster home. Foster carers must be prepared to help make these visits as easy as possible, in spite of all the uncertainties. Sometimes part of

> **I enjoy working with the adults as much as the child. If I had my own children and I was at home with them all day, it would drive me mad. But you go to meetings and get involved with the plans and decisions and you're always working towards things. It's brilliant.**
> Foster carer, in *Growing up in Foster Care*

the task is helping the parent learn to care for the child. Other relatives, like brothers or sisters or grandparents, may also keep in touch with the child, and foster carers need to encourage this.

Are there different kinds of fostering?

Yes. Some parents make private arrangements for their children to be looked after by private foster carers who are not approved and registered with the local authority. There are special regulations for private fostering (see Useful Reading). However, the majority of foster children are looked after by local authorities. These agencies work with parents to make plans for the children. Their parents may have asked for them to be looked after, or a court may have ordered that a local authority should share responsibility with their parents. In Scotland, a Children's Hearing may have made a supervision requirement, with a condition that the children reside with foster carers. Also, in Scotland, the court may have granted a Parental Responsibilities Order to the local authority giving them almost all parental responsibilities and rights and the local authority may have the child looked after by foster carers.

There are a number of specialist fostering schemes which your local authority or a neighbouring one may run. For example, some children need very temporary care, but on a regular basis, perhaps one or two weekends a month. This is often called respite care or short break care. Other children and young people need family care

> **We just love having children around. We've got a grown-up daughter and two teenagers at home and we also foster. We like having groups of brothers and sisters and we've got three at the moment. They're aged two, four and five and their social worker has just found adopters for them which is great, although we'll miss them!**
> Foster carer

following a court appearance and this is often called remand fostering.

| Could I foster a baby?

You can say which age children you would prefer to foster and, if you prefer to look after babies or small children, you should say so. But it is important to remember that fostering is not a way into adopting a baby or young child. You will be expected to care for the child on a short term basis until he or she returns home or until other plans are made.

| Fostering and adoption

The majority of fostered children are able to return to their birth families. Many children need help for only a few days or weeks, but others may stay for months or even several years while permanent plans are made and carried out. For some children, adoption becomes the plan and foster carers have an important role in helping the child to move on to their new permanent family.

Fostering does not usually lead on to adoption. You have to get used to seeing a child leaving your home, a child you have grown to love. But it can be very satisfying – children who arrive frightened and upset can leave feeling much more confident. Helping a child move on is one of the most important tasks of foster carers.

Sometimes, however, there might be agreement between social services and yourself that it would be best for a particular child to remain with you or be adopted by you. This would need full and careful discussion and you would need to be re-assessed and approved as an adoptive parent. Currently in England, just over 400

> **I knew she only acted like that because that was the way she'd been treated herself. So we decided to keep her, because she'd had a rough deal – and she deserved a chance.**
> Jane, a foster carer, *Foster Care*, issue 25

children a year, or 14 per cent of all the looked after children adopted, are adopted by their foster carers. A recent survey in Scotland found that almost a third of children needing a permanent new family found this by remaining with their foster carers, some through adoption and others through long-term fostering.

If you have fostered a child for a year or more and you want to adopt, it is possible to notify the local authority of your intention to adopt and to apply to court for an Adoption Order. However, it is much better to work with the local authority if you can.

| Concurrent planning

This is the term given to a very small number of schemes currently operating. Children, usually babies or toddlers, for whom there is one last chance that they might return home to their birth family, are placed with families who will foster them with this aim. However, the foster carers are also approved as adopters and will keep the child, should the planned return home not be successful. In this way, the moves that a child may otherwise have to make are minimised. These schemes operate with the agreement of the local court and to tight timescales.

| What about long-term fostering?

Sometimes, particularly for children aged 10 or over, foster care may be the plan until the child grows up. This long-term fostering cannot provide the same legal security as adoption for either the child or the foster family, but it may be the right plan for some children.

Some older children may accept, reluctantly, that they will never be able to return home to live and that they need a new family. However, they may be clear that they do not want to be adopted. They may also need a lot of extra help, for example, special schooling, hospital appointments, regular therapy sessions. You may decide that you would like to work in partnership with the local authority to offer long-term fostering to a child or young person. The child would remain the legal responsibility of the local authority and of their birth parents. For some children in Scotland, the local authority will have obtained a Parental Responsibilities Order, giving it almost all parental responsibilities and rights. You would receive a regular fostering allowance as well as being able to call on the local authority for help and support. You need to understand that most of the children for whom long-term fostering is the plan are at least nine or 10 years old.

What kind of people become foster carers?

Many different kinds of people are able to give children a loving and secure foster home. Some foster carers have young children of their own; some are older people whose children are now adults; others may not have any children of their own. Some are couples and others are single. Some people foster one child at a time, others more than one; some foster only babies or toddlers, others particularly like to look after teenagers. Foster carers come from all walks of life and live in all kinds of homes. It is the job of the social worker in the local authority or child care agency to find the right foster carers for each child, and this includes considering cultural and religious factors, among others.

Would I get paid?

Parents make their own arrangements about payment for private fostering, but when children are looked after by local authorities, foster carers are paid an allowance. This allowance covers the cost of feeding, clothing and looking after the child. Fostering allowances vary from area to area and according to the age and needs of the child.

> **Always remember that you can make a real difference. It can be very traumatic, but it can also be very rewarding – and when you remember that a little bit of upset for you can change their entire life, you realise that it really is worth it.**
> Foster carer, *Foster Care*, issue 13

Sometimes, foster carers are paid more than just their allowances for looking after a child. They can be paid a fee in recognition of their particular skills and/or because the child whom they are fostering has special needs.

How would I go about fostering a child?

First of all, you need to contact a fostering agency covering your area. This could be your local Social Services Department (England and Wales) or Social Work Department (Scotland) or Health and Social Services Trust (Northern Ireland). It could also be a neighbouring one although, as children are usually placed as close as possible to their home area, it is a good idea to apply to an agency as close as possible to where you live. You need to ask to speak to someone on the fostering team.

Voluntary organisations and independent fostering agencies also recruit, assess and approve families for fostering.

Details of all fostering agencies are on BAAF's website and in the BAAF book *Fostering a Child* (see Useful Reading).

How would I get approved to foster?

Most agencies run preparation and training groups for prospective foster carers as well as meeting with you individually. The whole family will need to be involved. If you have birth children, they will need a chance to think about what fostering will mean for them. Confidential enquiries will be made of your local authority and the police and you will probably be asked to have a medical examination. The fostering agency to which you have applied will prepare a report, with your help, on your application. This report is presented to the agency's fostering panel, a group of up to ten people, who include social workers and independent members and at least one foster carer. You should be invited to meet the panel if you wish. The panel makes a recommendation on your application and this goes to a senior manager in the agency who makes the final decision. This process usually takes several months. National Standards in Scotland suggest that it should not take more than six months from the completion of the application form.

| ## What support would I get?

The fostering agency must make a foster care agreement with you when you are approved. This covers expectations of both parties and includes the requirement, laid down in regulations, that you should not administer corporal punishment.

As a foster carer, you have to work closely with the child's social worker as well as with the child's birth family. In the early stages this will ensure that you know everything possible about the child, his or her likes and dislikes, normal routine, favourite foods and toys, etc. Later you will need to discuss the child's progress regularly with the worker and help plan for his or her future.

The local authority must keep records of foster children and foster carers. The local authority and foster carers must make a foster placement agreement, when a child is placed, about matters such as the arrangements for the child's health needs to be met, contact with the birth family and financial support for the child. The local authority must provide foster carers with written information about such things as the child's background, health, and mental and emotional development.

As well as having regular visits from the social workers for the children whom you are fostering, you will have your own supervising social worker, who is there to support and help you in

> **Getting the training in managing difficult behaviour was a big help. We had this lad who was – I don't know, up and down all the time. Like a pot boiler. After the training I had these new ideas and more confidence, and some of them really worked for him!**
> Barry, foster carer

the fostering task. Foster carers are usually also offered regular ongoing training and there may also be a programme of social events where you and your family can meet other foster families.

The children whom you foster will have regular reviews, a month after placement, three months after that and then at least every six months. You will be involved in these and your input will be important. All foster carers are also required to have their approval reviewed every year and this provides an opportunity for you to comment on the support you have had.

| Special guardianship

This is a new order, introduced under the Adoption and Children Act 2002, from 30 December 2005 in England and Wales. In terms of legal security it fits between adoption and a residence order. Birth parents do not lose their parental responsibility and so there is still a legal link between the child and them. However, the special guardian acquires parental responsibility which they are able to exercise to the exclusion of others with parental responsibility in all but a very few instances (for example, agreement to a change of name or to adoption).

Special guardians whose child was looked after by the local authority before the order was made are entitled to ask to be assessed for a range of support services, including financial support. These support services are very similar to those available to adoptive parents.

Special guardianship is seen as being appropriate when a child or young person and their birth parents do not want to lose the legal link between them but where it is agreed that the child needs permanent new parents who will make all the day-to-day decisions about their care and upbringing. It may be more appropriate than adoption in some situations where children are being permanently cared for by relatives. Special guardianship orders can be revoked by a court and so, while giving more legal security that a residence order or long-term fostering, do not give the complete legal security of adoption.

If you are a foster carer and think that special guardianship might be appropriate you should talk to the child's social worker and/or to a solicitor with experience of child care law.

The process for applying is to notify the local authority in writing of your intention. Three months later you can apply to a Magistrates' Family Proceedings Court, the County Court or the High Court, provided the child has lived with you for at least one year. The local authority is required to prepare a report for the court. You should ensure as far as possible that your support needs are fully discussed and agreed at this stage, although you can apply for these to be further assessed after the order has been made, if necessary.

Residence Orders in England and Wales and Northern Ireland

The making of a Residence Order under the Children Act 1989 or Children's (NI) Order 1995 gives people looking after a child more day-to-day rights than foster carers have, but not as many as adopters or special guardians. The child is no longer looked after by the local authority but the birth parents are still legally involved. They retain their parental responsibility but the holders of a Residence Order acquire this too. Foster carers can apply for a Residence Order even if the child's parents or local authority are not in agreement, provided that the child has lived with them for at least 12 months. The local authority can pay a Residence Order allowance, but is not obliged to do so. A Residence Order usually lasts until the child is 18. If you want to know more about Residence Orders you should talk to your local Social Services Department or a solicitor with experience of child care law.

Residence Orders in Scotland

In Scotland, anyone, including foster carers, can apply for a Residence Order under section 11 of the Children (Scotland) Act 1995, if they can show that this is in the child's interests. A Residence

Order gives the carers parental responsibilities and rights but not as many as an Adoption Order would and without removing all the birth parent's responsibilities and rights. A Residence Order lasts until the child is 16. The local authority can pay a residence allowance but is not obliged to do so. Your local Social Work Department can tell you more about the orders.

| Further information

BAAF has a companion book to this one, *Fostering a Child*. This would probably be helpful for you if you think that fostering rather than adoption may be right for you.

Stepchildren and adoption

POSED BY MODELS

When my husband and I divorced, Jordan was only one-and-a-half and continued to live with me. A few years later I remarried and David and I had Julia. We really wanted the four of us to be a family. David wanted to adopt Jordan but, after talking this through with Jordan, who still saw her father regularly, we realised that this would not be right for her. We are now thinking of applying for a Residence Order.
Birth parent

England and Wales

You are a stepfamily if you or your partner have a child from a previous relationship who is living with you. It is estimated that there are as many as 2.5 million children in England and Wales living in stepfamilies at any one time. Only a small proportion of these children are adopted each year, about 1,800 children. However, these adoptions do account for almost one-third of all adoptions in England and Wales (the others being looked after children and children adopted from abroad).

Most stepfamilies don't adopt. The adults involved work out satisfactory arrangements for the care and upbringing of the children, who will often have contact with the family members with whom they are not living. However, if you are considering adoption, the following information may be helpful. You may also find it helpful to read the BAAF leaflet *Stepchildren and Adoption* (see Useful Reading).

> **Are there other ways to help make the child secure in our family?**

A parental responsibility agreement or order

The Adoption and Children Act 2002, which came into force on 30 December 2005, has introduced this new option for step-parents. It is available to a step-parent who is married to, or has entered into a civil registration with, the child's birth parent. A step-parent may acquire parental responsibility for the child by a simple but formal agreement with the parent who is his or her partner and with the other parent if he or she has parental responsibility. The agreement must be recorded on an official form and signed by each parent with parental responsibility and the step-parent, in front of a court official. Copies must be lodged at the Principal Registry of the Family Division. The official form and guidance notes can be obtained from the Court Service at www.hmcourts-service.gov.uk.

If the non-resident parent who has parental responsibility will not enter into this agreement an application can be made for a parental responsibility order to a Magistrates' Family Proceedings Court, the County Court or the High Court. There is no need to give prior notice to the local authority but the court may ask for a report about the child's welfare.

A parental responsibility agreement or order does not take parental responsibility away from parents who already have it.

A Residence Order (see Chapter 7)

This is a court order which sets out with whom the child is to reside (or live). It also gives the step-parent who acquires it parental responsibility for the child. However, it doesn't take parental responsibility away from anyone else who has it, for example, the child's mother or the non-resident father if the parents were married when the child was born or if he has acquired parental responsibility. In effect, the child would have three parents with responsibility for ensuring his or her welfare. A step-parent does not need to be married to, or in a civil partnership with, the child's parent before applying for a Residence Order. You can apply for a Residence Order to your local Magistrates' Family Proceedings Court, the County Court or the High Court. It wouldn't prevent you applying for an Adoption Order at a later stage if you wish.

It is also important for the parent with whom the child is living to make a will, appointing a guardian for the child in the event of his or her death. If the step-parent is appointed and has a Residence Order, the child will stay with him or her should their birth parent die.

> **We'd like the child to
> have the same surname
> as us**

You don't have to adopt the child to achieve this. If the child's parents were married or the father has acquired parental responsibility, the child's surname cannot be changed without the agreement of the non-resident parent, unless a court gives permission. However, if the child's parents were not married and the father does not have parental responsibility, the child's surname can be changed with the agreement of his or her mother either by common usage or by a statutory declaration or by deed poll. You would need to consult a citizen's advice bureau or solicitor about this. Obviously your child's wishes should be taken into account. Many children now live in families where there are a number of different surnames and they may be quite happy with this and want to retain their own birth surname.

Does the child's other parent have to be contacted and agree to an Adoption or Residence Order?

If the other parent is the mother, or is a father who was married to the child's mother or who has acquired parental responsibility, his or her agreement to an Adoption or Residence Order is necessary. A court considering an application can dispense with the parent's agreement but would need compelling reasons to do so. If the child's birth father was not married to the mother and does not have parental responsibility, his formal agreement is not necessary. However, the court would want to know what his views were and would usually require efforts to have been made to seek these. The court would consider the father's views in relation to the part he has played, or wished to play, in the child's life.

Does the child have to know what is happening?

Yes. The court will want to know what the child's views are. This would apply to children of four or so, and older. The court would want assurances that younger children will be told the truth about their parentage and about the adoption. This should usually start from when the child is about three, so that they grow up always having known.

Do we have to be married to adopt?

No, the Adoption and Children Act 2002, which came into force on 30 December 2005, no longer requires the step-parent to be married to their partner. However, they must have been living with them and the child for at least six months. The step-parent can apply for an Adoption Order and, if granted, this will give him or her the same parental rights as their partner, the resident birth parent, while taking away the parental responsibility and rights of any parent or other person who previously had this.

What is the process for applying to adopt?

You must notify the local authority where you live of your intention to adopt. It can be useful to arrange to speak to a social worker in Social Services to discuss whether adoption will be a good plan. If you decide to go ahead, you must wait three months after notifying the local authority of your intention and then you need to apply to a local Magistrates' Family Proceedings Court, to a County Court or to the High Court. There will be a fee to pay and you will need to complete an application form. The court will require a social worker in the local authority to produce a full report, called an Annex A report, for the court hearing. This will involve interviews with you both, with your children and with the other parent and this process should start once you notify the local authority of your intention to apply to adopt. On the basis of this report, the court will decide whether or not to make an Adoption Order. This process need not take longer than about three months, but can often take up to a year, depending on the circumstances of the case and the workload of the Social Services Department and the court.

Scotland

The situation is similar in that most stepfamilies do not adopt, although these adoptions do account for about a half of all adoptions in Scotland. As in England and Wales, a Residence Order can be a good alternative and can give the child some security and the step-parent considerable responsibilities and rights. There are some differences in the law and in procedures in Scotland.

Change of name

There is a procedure whereby you can apply to change a name through the local Registrar's Office. You have to show that the child has been known by that name for at least two years. Your local Registrar's Office can help you with this.

Your child's views about adoption

The law requires that the child's own wishes and feelings are taken into account, as in England and Wales. However, in Scotland a child of 12 or over will be asked formally if she or he consents to the adoption.

Do I have to adopt my own child with my new partner?

No. A step-parent in Scotland is able to adopt the child on his or her own with the consent of the birth parent to whom he or she must be married.

Is the consent of the non-resident birth parent necessary?

Yes, if this is the mother or a father who has parental responsibilities and rights. If such a birth parent is in disagreement with the adoption, then the court can be asked to dispense with that agreement. There will need to be a proof hearing before the Sheriff. In this situation you would be well advised to use a solicitor.

What is the process for applying to adopt?

Petitions are usually lodged with the local Sheriff Court. You also have to notify the local authority where you live that you intend to apply for an Adoption Order.

When the court receives your application, it will appoint a curator *ad litem*, an independent person, who will meet with you and your child and prepare a report for the court. A social worker from your local authority will also visit you to discuss the application and will prepare a separate report for the court.

9

Finding an adoption agency

Unless you are a close relative of the child you want to adopt, you must apply to an adoption agency. There are nearly 250 adoption agencies in England, Scotland, Wales and Northern Ireland. Most of these are based in local authority Social Services Departments in England and Wales or Social Work Departments in Scotland. In Northern Ireland, social services are provided by Health and Social Services Trusts commissioned by four Health and Social Services Boards. These are listed in the following pages under the name of the county, borough or council, or Health Board.

There are also voluntary adoption agencies: Barnardo's is an example. Some of these are linked to churches, for example, the Catholic Children's Society. On the whole, all agencies work with applicants of any religious faith or none.

Local authority adoption agencies covering large areas tend to take applications mainly from people within their area. However, agencies which are geographically small, for example, London boroughs, often prefer not to recruit adopters from their own area as they will tend to live too close to the birth families of the children who need placement.

Voluntary adoption agencies usually cover a wider area than the local authorities do, often covering several counties. So it is worth contacting voluntary adoption agencies in counties near to your own, as well as any in it.

You are not limited to your own immediate locality, but most agencies work roughly within a 50-mile radius of their office. It is important to remember that you and your child will need help and support from the agency after placement. It is much harder for an agency to give you adequate support if they are based a long way away and you should discuss what their plans are for this before you decide to work with them.

Would it be best to apply to the local authority or to a voluntary adoption agency?

Voluntary agencies tend to be small and to specialise in adoption and fostering work. They are often able to give very good support once a child is placed with you. Local authorities are bigger and have to respond to a wide range of needs. However, they are the agencies responsible for placing children and will consider families whom they have approved first. They may expect you to wait for up to three months after you are approved for the placement of a child looked after by them before referring you to the Adoption Register for England and Wales and before you respond to children from other local authorities whom you may see needing a new family. Voluntary agencies will actively help you to try and find a child, through using the Adoption Register for England and Wales, *Be My Parent* or *Adoption Today* and other contacts. So, there can be advantages and disadvantages in working with either type of agency. (Please note that it is only adoption agencies in England and Wales which can refer families and children to the Adoption Register.)

What they are looking for

All the adoption agencies listed in the following pages are looking for permanent new families for school-age children, disabled children or those with learning disabilities or difficulties, and for groups of brothers and sisters. There are some black babies and toddlers who, like all other children, need parents of the same ethnicity as themselves. If you are white and would like to adopt a baby or toddler without disabilities you can contact agencies, but you must be prepared to find that lists may be closed.

British Association for Adoption & Fostering

The British Association for Adoption & Fostering (BAAF) has close links with most of the adoption agencies listed in this book. You are welcome to contact us for advice about the adoption process and about finding an agency. However, we do not take up adoption applications ourselves. We have several regional and country offices in the UK, and we have included the address and telephone number of these on the following pages.

How to find an adoption agency

On the next few pages, you will find lists of local authority and voluntary agencies in England, Scotland, Wales and Northern Ireland. These are divided into five different groups; each of these is served by BAAF offices located in that area. However, currently there is no BAAF office in Northern Ireland. BAAF expects to open one from April 2006 (check www.baaf.org.uk for updates) but until that time, enquiries should go to the Southern Region office in London.

When you have found the name of one or more agencies that are reasonably near you, you can phone or write for further information. Agencies may also have a website which you can visit. Guidance to the Adoption and Children Act 2002 states that you should expect to receive written information in response to your enquiry within five working days (seven in Scotland). You can contact a number of agencies at this early stage. However, you can make a firm application and enter into the preparation and assessment process with only one agency.

Unfortunately, we have not been able to include particular details about each of the agencies, for example, whether the agency occasionally needs families for white babies or whether it has a religious interest. A phone call to the agency will of course give you the necessary details. Your BAAF centre will also be able to help you. BAAF's website enables you to find some information about the agency – you can find this on www.baaf.org.uk/res/agencydb/index.shtm.

ENGLAND: CENTRAL AND NORTHERN

BAAF REGIONAL OFFICES

Dolphin House
54 Coventry Road
Coleshill
BIRMINGHAM
B10 0RX
Tel: 0121 753 2001
Email: midlands@baaf.org.uk

Unit 4
Pavilion Business Park
Royds Hall Road
Wortley
LEEDS
LS12 6AJ
Tel: 0113 274 4797
Email: leeds@baaf.org.uk

and

MEA House
Ellison Place
NEWCASTLE UPON TYNE
NE1 8XS
Tel: 0191 261 6600
Email: newcastle@baaf.org.uk

BAAF
North West

Jane Asquith
PO Box 96
WELLINGTON
Shropshire
TF6 6WA
Tel/Fax: 01952 771222
Email: north.west@baaf.org.uk

LOCAL AUTHORITY OFFICES

BARNSLEY METROPOLITAN
BOROUGH COUNCIL
Adoption and Fostering Unit
Wellington House, 36 Wellington Street
BARNSLEY
South Yorkshire
S70 1WA
Tel: 01226 775876
Email: adoptionandfostering@
barnsley.gov.uk
www.barnsley.gov.uk

BIRMINGHAM CITY COUNCIL
The Family Finding Team
Silvermere Centre
Silvermere Road
Sheldon

BIRMINGHAM
B26 3XA
Tel: 0121 303 8400
www.birmingham.gov.uk

BLACKBURN WITH DARWEN COUNCIL
Social Services Department
Link 36
The Exchange
Ainsworth Street
BLACKBURN
BB1 6AD
Tel: 01254 666806
www.blackburn.gov.uk

BLACKPOOL BOROUGH COUNCIL
Children and Young People's
Department
Social Care Division
Progress House, Clifton Road
BLACKPOOL
FY4 4US
Tel: 01253 477888
www.blackpool.gov.uk

BOLTON METROPOLITAN BOROUGH COUNCIL
Social Services Department
Endeavour House
90 Waters Meeting Road
The Valley
BOLTON
Lancashire
BL1 8SW
Tel: 01204 337480
www.bolton.gov.uk

BRADFORD CITY METROPOLITAN DISTRICT COUNCIL
Adoption and Fostering Unit
35 Saltaire Road
SHIPLEY

West Yorkshire
BD18 3HH
Tel: 01274 137343
www.bradford.gov.uk

BURY METROPOLITAN COUNCIL
Social Services Department
Family Placement Department
18 – 20 St Mary's Place
BURY
Lancashire
BL9 0DZ
Tel: 0161 253 5457
www.bury.gov.uk

CALDERDALE COUNCIL
Family Placement Team
Ovenden Hall, Ovenden Road
HALIFAX
West Yorkshire
HX3 5QG
Tel: 01422 353279
www.calderdale.gov.uk

CHESHIRE COUNTY COUNCIL
Family Placement Support Services
Goldsmith House, Hamilton Place
CHESTER
CH1 1SE
Tel: 01244 602222
www.fosteringincheshire.co.uk

COVENTRY CITY COUNCIL SOCIAL SERVICES DEPARTMENT
Family Placement Service
Old Stoke House, Lloyd Crescent
Stoke Hill Estate
COVENTRY
CV2 5NY
Tel: 02476 659009
www.cov.gov.uk

CUMBRIA COUNTY COUNCIL
Social Services Department
Adoption Unit

3 Alfred Street North
CARLISLE
CA1 1PX
Tel: 01228 607191 or 607109

DARLINGTON COUNCIL
Social Services Department
Fostering Team, Central House
Gladstone Street
DARLINGTON
Co Durham
DL3 6JX
Tel: 01325 346452
www.darlington.gov.uk

DERBY CITY COUNCIL
Children and Young People Adoption
Service
Chaddesden Office
Perth Street
Chaddesden
DERBY
DE21 6XX
Tel: 01332 717741
www.derby.gov.uk

DERBYSHIRE COUNTY COUNCIL
Derbyshire Adoption Service
County Hall
MATLOCK
Derbyshire
DE4 3AG
Tel: 01629 772205
www.derbyshire.gov.uk

**DONCASTER METROPOLITAN
BOROUGH COUNCIL**
The Adoption Team
PO Box 251
The Council House
College Road
DONCASTER
South Yorkshire
DN1 3DA

Tel: 01302 736968 or 737059
Email: adoption@doncaster.gov.uk
www.doncaster.gov.uk

**DUDLEY METROPOLITAN
BOROUGH COUNCIL**
Social Services Department
Ednam House
1 St James's Road
DUDLEY
West Midlands
DY1 3JJ
Tel: 01384 815891
www.dudley.gov.uk

DURHAM COUNTY COUNCIL
Durham Resource Centre
Fostering and Adoption
Littleburn Business Centre
Mill Road
Langley Moore
DURHAM
DH7 8ET
Tel: 0191 370 6100
www.durham.gov.uk

**EAST RIDING OF YORKSHIRE
COUNCIL**
Childcare Resources
31/31A Lairgate
BEVERLEY
HU17 8ET
Tel: 01482 396644
www.eastriding.gov.uk

**GATESHEAD METROPOLITAN
BOROUGH COUNCIL**
The Adoption Team
Gateshead Council
Council Offices
Prince Consort Road
GATESHEAD
NE8 4UJ
Tel: 0191 433 8333

Email: adoptionandfostering@
gateshead.gov.uk
www.gatesheadgov.uk

HALTON BOROUGH COUNCIL
Adoption and Fostering Team
Grosvenor House
Halton Lea
RUNCORN
WA7 2ED
Tel: 01928 704360
www.halton.gov.uk

HARTLEPOOL BOROUGH COUNCIL
The Placement Team
Children's Services
Aneurin Bevan House
35 Avenue Road
HARTLEPOOL
TS24 8HD
Tel: 01429 523929

HEREFORDSHIRE COUNCIL
The Children's Resource Team
Moor House
Widemarsh Common
HEREFORD
HR4 9NA
Tel: 01432 262835
www.herefordshire.gov.uk

HULL CITY COUNCIL
Adoption Services
Children and Young People's Centre
East Car Road
HULL
HU8 9LB
Tel: 01482 799340
www.hullcc.gov.uk

ISLE OF MAN GOVERNMENT
Adoption Service
3 Albany Lane

DOUGLAS
Isle of Man
IM2 3NS
Tel: 01624 625161
www.mcaws.org.im

KIRKLEES METROPOLITAN COUNCIL
Family Placement Unit
Westfields, Westfields Road
MIRFIELD
WF14 9PW
Tel: 01924 483707
www.kirklees.gov.uk

KNOWSLEY METROPOLITAN BOROUGH COUNCIL
Social Services Department
Adoption and Fostering Services
Astley House, Astley Road
HUYTON
L36 8HY
Tel: 0151 443 3958
www.knowsley.gov.uk

LANCASHIRE COUNTY COUNCIL
Children and Young Persons
County Hall
PRESTON
Lancashire
PR1 0LD
Tel: 01772 534273
www.lancashire.gov.uk

LEEDS CITY COUNCIL
Social Services Department
Fostering and Adoption
3rd Floor West, Merrion House
110 Merrion Centre
LEEDS
LS2 8QB
Tel: 0113 247 4747
www.leeds.gov.uk

**LEICESTER CITY COUNCIL/
LEICESTERSHIRE COUNTY
COUNCIL/ RUTLAND COUNTY
COUNCIL**
Joint Adoption Team
Eagle House
11 Friar Lane
LEICESTER
LE1 5RB
Tel: 0116 299 5899
www.leicester.gov.uk

**LINCOLNSHIRE COUNTY
COUNCIL**
Orchard House
Orchard Street
LINCOLN
LN1 1BA
Tel: 01522 554060 or
Freephone: 0800 093 3099
www.family-lincs.org.uk

CITY OF LIVERPOOL
Fostering and Adoption Team
Parklands Customer Focus Centre
Conleach Road
Speke
LIVERPOOL
L24 0TY
Tel: 0151 233 3029
www.liverpool.gov.uk

MANCHESTER CITY COUNCIL
Chorlton Social Services Office
102 Manchester Road
Chorlton
MANCHESTER
M21 9SZ
Tel: 0161 860 7666 or 0161 881 0911
www.manchester.gov.uk

**MIDDLESBROUGH BOROUGH
COUNCIL**
Middlesbrough Teaching and Learning
Centre

Tranmere Avenue
MIDDLESBROUGH
TS3 8PD
Tel: 01642 201962/965
www.middlesbrough.gov.uk

NEWCASTLE CITY COUNCIL
Adoption Team
Room 26
Shieldfield Centre
4–8 Clarence Walk, Shieldfield
NEWCASTLE UPON TYNE
NE2 1AL
Tel: 0191 278 8200
www.newcastle.gov.uk

**NORTHAMPTONSHIRE COUNTY
COUNCIL**
Adoption Services
Norborough House
Coverack Close
NORTHAMPTON
NN4 8PQ
Tel: 01604 704704
www.northamptonshire.gov.uk

**NORTH EAST LINCOLNSHIRE
COUNCIL**
Adoption Service
2nd Floor, St James House
St James Square
GRIMSBY
DN31 1EP
Tel: 01472 325555
www.nelincs.gov.uk

**NORTH LINCOLNSHIRE
COUNCIL**
Adoption and Fostering Team
The Grove
38 West Street
SCAWBY
Near Brigg
North Lincs
DN20 9AN

Tel: 01652 656005
www.northlincs.gov.uk

NORTH TYNESIDE COUNCIL
Children's Services
Adoption Team
Camden House
Camden Street
NORTH SHIELDS
Tyne and Wear
NE30 1NW
Tel: 0191 200 8181
www.northtyneside.gov.uk/adoption

**NORTHUMBERLAND COUNTY
COUNCIL**
Family Placement and Support Service
Tweed House, Hepscott Park
Stannington
MORPETH
Northumberland
NE61 6NF
Tel: 01670 534450
Email: familysupport@
northumberland.gov.uk
www.northumberland.gov.uk

**NORTH YORKSHIRE COUNTY
COUNCIL**
Adoption Team
Jesmond House
31–33 Victoria Avenue
HARROGATE
HG1 5QE
Tel: 01609 779999 or 01423 561951
www.northyorks.gov.uk

NOTTINGHAM CITY COUNCIL
City Adoption Section
2nd Floor, York House
Mansfield Road
NOTTINGHAM
NG1 3NS

Tel: 0115 915 1721
www.nottinghamcity.gov.uk

**OLDHAM METROPOLITAN
BOROUGH COUNCIL**
Adoption Team
Unit 7–13 Whitney Court
Southlink Business Park
OLDHAM
OL4 1DB
Tel: 0161 626 4947
www.oldham.gov.uk/adoption

**REDCAR & CLEVELAND
BOROUGH COUNCIL**
Grosmont Resource Centre
20 Grosmont Close
REDCAR
Cleveland
TS10 4PJ
Tel: 01642 495910
www.redcar-cleveland.gov.uk

**ROCHDALE METROPOLITAN
BOROUGH COUNCIL**
Family Placement Team
Foxholes House, Foxholes Road
ROCHDALE
Lancashire
OL12 0ED
Tel: 01706 710750
www.rochdale.gov.uk

**ROTHERHAM BOROUGH
COUNCIL**
Family Placement Service
4th floor, Crinoline House
Effingham Square
ROTHERHAM
S65 1AW
Tel: 01709 382 121
www.rotherham.gov.uk

RUTLAND COUNTY COUNCIL
see under Leicester City

SALFORD CITY COUNCIL
Family Placement Section
Avon House
Avon Close, Little Hulton
MANCHESTER
M28 0LA
Tel: 0161 603 4300 or 799 1268
www.salford.gov.uk/adoption
andfostering

**SANDWELL METROPOLITAN
BOROUGH COUNCIL**
Family Placements
Crystal House
1/7 Crystal Drive
Sandwell Business Park
SMETHWICK
West Midlands
B56 1QG
Tel: 0845 352 8609
www.sandwell.gov.uk

**SEFTON METROPOLITAN
BOROUGH COUNCIL**
Children, Schools and Families
Department
Permanence, Adoption and Family
Placement Teams
Ellesmere House
Crosby Road North
Waterloo
LIVERPOOL
L22 0LG
Tel: 0151 285 5019 or 285 5018
www.sefton.gov.uk

**SHEFFIELD METROPOLITAN
CITY COUNCIL**
Family Placement Services
2nd Floor, Castle Market Buildings
Exchange Street
SHEFFIELD

S1 2AH
Tel: 0114 273 5075
www.sheffield.gov.uk

**SHROPSHIRE COUNTY COUNCIL/
TELFORD & WREKIN COUNCIL**
Joint Adoption Team
Children and Young People's Services
Shirehall
Abbey Foregate
SHREWSBURY
Shropshire
SY2 6BL
Tel: 01743 241915
www.shropshireonline.gov.uk

**SOLIHULL METROPOLITAN
BOROUGH COUNCIL**
Adoption and Placements Team
Education and Children's Services
Jubilee House
655 Auckland Drive
Smith's Wood
SOLIHULL
B36 0SN
Tel: 0121 749 8100
www.solihull.gov.uk

**SOUTH TYNESIDE
METROPOLITAN BOROUGH
COUNCIL**
Adoption Section
16 Barrington Street
SOUTH SHIELDS
Tyne & Wear
NE33 1AN
Tel: 0191 423 8500
www.southtyneside.info/fosteringand
adoption

**STAFFORDSHIRE COUNTY
COUNCIL**
Children and Lifelong Learning
Directorate
Walton Building

PO Box 11, Martin Street
STAFFORD
ST16 2LH
Tel: 01785 277033 or
Family Placement Team
Stafford Area Office
Madford Retail Park
Foregate Street
STAFFORD
ST16 2PA
Freephone: 0800 169 2061
www.staffordshire.gov.uk

**ST HELENS METROPOLITAN
BOROUGH COUNCIL**
Adoption and Foster Care Services
73 Corporation Street
ST HELENS
Merseyside
WA10 1SX
Tel: 01744 456526
www.sthelens.gov.uk/adoption

**STOCKPORT METROPOLITAN
BOROUGH COUNCIL**
Children and Young People's Directorate
Reddish Green Centre
St Elizabeth's Way
Reddish
STOCKPORT
SK5 6BL
Tel: 0161 442 2055
www.stockport.gov.uk

**STOCKTON-ON-TEES BOROUGH
COUNCIL**
Billingham Council Offices
Town Centre
BILLINGHAM
Stockton on Tees
Cleveland
TS23 2LW
Tel: 01642 526218
www.stockton.gov.uk

**STOKE ON TRENT CITY
COUNCIL**
Adoption Team
Heron Cross House, Grove Road
Fenton
STOKE ON TRENT
ST4 3AY
Tel: 01782 234555
www.stoke.gov.uk

CITY OF SUNDERLAND
Services for Looked After Children
Penshaw House, Station Road
Penshaw
HOUGHTON-LE-SPRING
DH4 7LB
Tel: 0191 382 3108
www.sunderland.gov.uk

**TAMESIDE METROPOLITAN
BOROUGH COUNCIL**
Social Care and Health Department
Adoption and Permanency Team
56 Warrington Street
ASHTON-UNDER-LYNE
OL6 7JX
Tel: 0161 342 4150
www.tameside.gov.uk

**TRAFFORD METROPOLITAN
BOROUGH COUNCIL**
Children and Young People's Services
The Resource Centre
71A Northenden Road
SALE
Cheshire
N33 2DG
Tel: 0161 912 3971
www.trafford.gov.uk

**CITY OF WAKEFIELD
METROPOLITAN DISTRICT
COUNCIL**
Social Services Department
Family Placement Services

Flanshaw Children's Centre
6 Springfield Grange
Flanshaw
WAKEFIELD
WF2 9QP
Tel: 01924 302160
www.wakefield.gov.uk

WALSALL METROPOLITAN BOROUGH COUNCIL
Children's Services, Adoption Team
Floor 1, Pinfold Health Centre
Field Road
Bloxwich
WALSALL
WS3 3JJ
Tel: 01922 775581
www.walsall.gov.uk

WARRINGTON BOROUGH COUNCIL
Fostering and Adoption Team
Family Placement Team
St Werburghs School, Irwell Road
WARRINGTON
WA4 6BB
Tel: 01925 444283 or 01925 457085
www.warrington.gov.uk

WARWICKSHIRE COUNTY COUNCIL
Fostering and Adoption Development Team
Farraday Hall
Lower Hillmorton Road
Hillmorton
RUGBY
CV21 3TU
Tel: 01926 413313
www.warwickshire.gov.uk

WIGAN METROPOLITAN BOROUGH COUNCIL
Social Services Department
Family Placement Team

Hesketh Meadow
196 Newton Road
Lowton
Nr. WARRINGTON
WA3 2AQ
Tel: 01942 487203/204
Email: ssdpermanence@
wigan.mbc.gov.uk
www.wiganmbc.gov.uk

WIRRAL METROPOLITAN BOROUGH COUNCIL
Adoption Team
Social Services Centre
Conway Buildings, Conway Street
off Burlington Street
BIRKENHEAD
Merseyside
CH41 6LA
Tel: 0151 666 4696

WOLVERHAMPTON CITY COUNCIL
Family Placement Service
Children's Services, Beldray Buildings
66 Mount Pleasant, Bilston
WOLVERHAMPTON
WV14 7PR
Tel: 01902 553070 or
Freephone: 0800 073 0189
www.wolverhampton.gov.uk

WORCESTERSHIRE COUNTY COUNCIL
Adoption and Fostering Development Team
Social Services Training Centre
Tolladine Road
WORCESTER
WR4 9NB
Tel: 0800 028 2158
www.worcestershire.gov.uk

YORK CITY COUNCIL
Children's Services

Adoption and Fostering
Hollycroft
Wenlock Terrace
Fulford Road
YORK
YO10 4DU
Tel: 01904 613161
www.york.gov.uk

VOLUNTARY AGENCIES

ADOPTION MATTERS
14 Liverpool Road
CHESTER
CH2 1AE
Tel: 01244 390938
Email: info@adoptionmatters.org
www.adoptionmatters.org

BARNARDO'S MIDLANDS NEW FAMILIES
Owen House
Little Cornbow
HALESOWEN
West Midlands
B63 3AJ
Tel: 0121 550 4737
Email: midlands.newfamilies@
barnardos.org.uk
www.barnardos.org.uk

BARNARDO'S NEW FAMILIES PROJECT
43 Briggate
Shipley
BRADFORD
West Yorkshire
BD17 7BP
Tel: 01274 532852
Email: newfamilies.yorkshire@
barnardos.org.uk
www.barnardos.org.uk

BARNARDO'S NEWCASTLE NEW FAMILIES
Barnardo's North East
Orchard House
Buston Terrace
Jesmond
NEWCASTLE UPON TYNE
NE2 2JL
Tel: 0191 281 5024
www.barnardos.org.uk

BLACKBURN DIOCESAN ADOPTION AGENCY
St Mary's House
Cathedral Close
BLACKBURN
BB1 5AA
Tel: 01254 57759
www.bdaa.org.uk

CATHOLIC CARE (DIOCESE OF LEEDS)
11 North Grange Road
Headingley
LEEDS
LS6 2BR
Tel: 0113 388 5400
Email: adoption@catholic-care.org.uk
www.catholic-care.org.uk

CATHOLIC CARING SERVICES TO CHILDREN & COMMUNITY (LANCASTER)
218 Tulketh Road
Ashton
PRESTON
Lancashire
PR2 1ES
Tel: 01772 732313

**CATHOLIC CHILDREN'S
SOCIETY (NOTTINGHAMSHIRE)**
7 Colwick Road
West Bridgford
NOTTINGHAM
NG2 5GR
Tel: 0115 955 8811
Email: enquiries@ccsnotts.co.uk
www.ccsnotts.co.uk

**CATHOLIC CHILDREN'S RESCUE
SOCIETY (DIOCESE OF
SALFORD) INC**
390 Parrs Wood Road
Didsbury
MANCHESTER
M20 5NA
Tel: 0161 445 7741
www.ccrsorg.co.uk

**CATHOLIC CHILDREN'S
SOCIETY (DIOCESE OF
SHREWSBURY)**
St Paul's House
Farmfield Drive
Beechwood
PRENTON
Wirral
CH43 7ZT
Tel: 0151 652 1281
www.cathchildsoc.org.uk

CORAM FAMILY
Lacey Court
Charn Wood Road
Shepshed
LOUGHBOROUGH
Leicestershire
LE12 9QY
Tel: 01509 600306
www.coram.org.uk

**DONCASTER ADOPTION &
FAMILY WELFARE SOCIETY LTD**
Jubilee House
1 Jubilee Road
Wheatley
DONCASTER
South Yorkshire
DN1 2UE
Tel: 01302 349909

DFW ADOPTION
Agriculture House
Stonebridge
DURHAM
DH1 3RY
Tel: 0191 386 3719
www.dfw-adoption.org

FATHER HUDSON'S SOCIETY
Coventry Road
Coleshill
BIRMINGHAM
B46 3EB
Tel: 01675 434020
Email: enquiries@frhudsons.org.uk
www.fatherhudsonssociety.org.uk

**THE ISLE OF MAN ADOPTION
SERVICE**
3 Albany Lane
DOUGLAS, ISLE OF MAN
IM2 3NS
Tel: 01624 625161 or 678301
www.mcaws.org.im

LDS FAMILY SERVICES (UK) LTD
399 Garretts Green Lane
Garretts Green
BIRMINGHAM
B33 0UH
Tel: 0121 785 4994
www.lds.org

**MANCHESTER ADOPTION
SOCIETY**
47 Bury New Road
Sedgley Park
MANCHESTER
M25 9JY
Tel: 0161 773 0973
www.manchesteradoption.com

NUGENT CARE SOCIETY
Children's Fieldwork Services
Blackbrook House
Blackbrook Road
St Helens
MERSEYSIDE
WA11 9RJ
Tel: 01744 605700
Email: fieldwork.services@
nugentcare.org
www.nugentcare.co.uk

ADOPTION NCH MIDLANDS
141 Wood End Lane
Erdington
BIRMINGHAM
B24 8BD
Tel: 0121 377 7999
Email: adoption.midlands@nch.org.uk
www.nch.org.uk

ADOPTION NCH YORKSHIRE
11 Queen Square
LEEDS
LS2 8AJ
Tel: 0113 242 9631
Email: neape@nch.org.uk
www.nch.org.uk

**SOUTHWELL DIOCESAN
COUNCIL FOR FAMILY CARE**
Warren House
2 Pelham Court
Pelham Road
NOTTINGHAM
NG5 1AP
Tel: 0115 960 3010
Email: info@familycare-
nottingham.org.uk
www.familycare-nottingham.org.uk

ENGLAND: SOUTHERN

BAAF SOUTHERN REGION

Saffron House
6 – 10 Kirby Street
LONDON
EC1N 8TS
Tel: 020 7421 2670/71
Email: southern@baaf.org.uk
www.baaf.org.uk

LOCAL AUTHORITY AGENCIES

BARKING AND DAGENHAM, LONDON BOROUGH OF
Children and Families Division
Placement Services
512A Heathway
DAGENHAM
Essex
RM10 7SL
Tel: 020 8227 5818
www.lbbd.gov.uk

BARNET, LONDON BOROUGH OF
Children and Families Division
6th Floor, Barnet House
1255 High Road
Whetstone
LONDON
N20 0EJ
Tel: 020 8359 5701
www.barnet.gov.uk

BATH & NORTH EAST SOMERSET COUNCIL
Family Placement
Social and Housing Services
PO Box 3343
BATH
BA1 2ZH
Tel: 01225 395332
www.bathnes.gov.uk

BEDFORDSHIRE COUNTY COUNCIL
Adoption and Family Finding Team
Social Services Department
Houghton Lodge, Houghton Close
(off Oliver Street)
AMPTHILL
Bedfordshire
MK45 2TG
Tel: 01525 840543
www.bedfordshire.gov.uk

BEXLEY COUNCIL
Social Services Department
Howbury Centre
Slade Green Road
ERITH
Kent
DA8 2HX
Tel: 020 8303 7777 Ext 3831
Email: adoption&fostering@
bexley.gov.uk
www.bexley.gov.uk

BOURNEMOUTH BOROUGH COUNCIL
Adoption Services
Social Services Directorate
North Bournemouth Local Office
27 Slades Farm Road
Ensbury Park
BOURNEMOUTH
BH10 4ES
Tel: 01202 456743
Email: adoption@bournemouth.gov.uk
www.bournemouth.gov.uk

BRACKNELL FOREST BOROUGH COUNCIL
Family Placement Team
Time Square
Market Street
BRACKNELL
Berkshire
RG12 1JD
Tel: 01344 351559
Email: family.placement@bracknell-
forest.gov.uk
www.bracknell.gov.uk

BRENT, LONDON BOROUGH OF
Children's Services and Social Care
Placements Team
Triangle House
328 – 330 High Road
WEMBLEY
HA9 6AZ

Tel: 020 8937 4558
www.brent.gov.uk

BRIGHTON & HOVE COUNCIL
Social Care and Health
253 Preston Road
BRIGHTON
BN1 6SE
Tel: 01273 295 4444
www.adoptioninbrightonandhove.org.uk

BRISTOL CITY COUNCIL
Social Services Department
Family Placement Team
PO Box 30, Amelia Court
Pipe Lane
BRISTOL
BS99 7NB
Tel: 0117 903 7782
www.bristol-city.gov.uk

BROMLEY, LONDON BOROUGH OF
Social Services Department
Joseph Lancaster Hall
Civic Centre
Rafford Way
BROMLEY
Kent
BR1 3UH
Tel: 020 8464 3333
www.bromley.gov.uk

BUCKINGHAMSHIRE COUNTY COUNCIL
Adoption Team
Council Offices
King George V Road
AMERSHAM
Buckinghamshire
HP6 5BN
Tel: 01494 729000
www.buckscc.gov.uk

CAMBRIDGESHIRE COUNTY COUNCIL
Fostering and Adoption Service
Buttsgrove Centre
38 Buttsgrove Way
HUNTINGDON
Cambridgeshire
PE29 1LY
Tel: 01480 376404
www.cambridgeshire.gov.uk

CAMDEN, LONDON BOROUGH OF
Permanent Placements Team
Gospel Oak Office
115 Wellesley Road
LONDON
NW5 4PA
Tel: 020 7974 6164/5
www.camden.gov.uk

CORNWALL COUNTY COUNCIL
Adoption and Family Finding Unit
13 Treyew Road
TRURO
Cornwall
TR1 2BY
Tel: 01872 270251
www.cornwall.gov.uk

CITY OF LONDON
Children and Families
Social Services Department
15 Half Moon Court
Bartholemew Close
LONDON
EC1A 7HF
Tel: 020 7332 3621
www.cityoflondon.gov.uk

CROYDON, LONDON BOROUGH OF
Fostering and Adoption Services
Fell Road
CROYDON
Surrey

CR9 1BQ
Tel: 020 8604 7726
www.croydon.gov.uk

DEVON COUNTY COUNCIL
Social Services
Parkers Barn
Parkers Way
TOTNES
Devon
TQ9 5UF
Tel: 01392 384848
Email: adoption@devon.gov.uk
www.devon.gov.uk

DORSET COUNTY COUNCIL
Adoption and Permanence Team
Acland Road
DORCHESTER
Dorset
DT1 1SH
Tel: 01305 251414
Email: dorchestersocialcare@
dorsetcc.gov.uk
www.dorsetcc.gov.uk

EALING, LONDON BOROUGH OF
Fostering and Adoption Connections
Acton Town Hall
Winchester Street
Acton
LONDON
W3 6NE
Tel: 0800 731 6550

EAST SUSSEX COUNTY COUNCIL
The County Adoption and Permanence
Team
6th Floor, St Mary's House
52 St Leonard's Road
EASTBOURNE
East Sussex
BN21 3UU
Tel: 01323 747154
www.eastsussex.gov.uk

ENFIELD, LONDON BOROUGH OF
Social Services Department
Triangle House
305 – 313 Green Lanes
Palmers Green
LONDON
N13 4YB
Tel: 020 8379 2846
www.enfield.gov.uk/adoption

ESSEX COUNTY COUNCIL
Adoption and Fostering Team
Social Services Department
125 – 127 New London Road
County Hall
CHELMSFORD
Essex
CM2 0QT
Tel: 0800 801530
www.essexcc.gov.uk

GLOUCESTERSHIRE COUNTY COUNCIL
The Adoption Team
Sandford House
39 – 41 London Road
CHELTENHAM
Gloucestershire
GL52 6XJ
Tel: 01242 532597
www.gloucestershire.gov.uk

GREENWICH, LONDON BOROUGH OF
Adoption Team
147 Powis Street
LONDON
SE18 6JL
Tel: 020 8921 2752
www.greenwichkids.org.uk

GUERNSEY, STATES OF
Homefinding and Befriending Service
Health and Social Services

Garden Hill Resource Centre
Rohais, St Peter Port
GUERNSEY
GY1 1FB
Tel: 01481 713230

HACKNEY, LONDON BOROUGH OF
Adoption and Fostering
205 Morning Lane
LONDON
E9 6JX
Tel: 08000 730418
Email: info@hackney.gov.uk
www.hackney.gov.uk/socialservices

HAMMERSMITH & FULHAM, LONDON BOROUGH OF
Family Placement Unit
2nd Floor, Barclay House
Effie Road
LONDON
SW6 1EN
Tel: 020 8748 3020
www.lbhs.gov.uk

HAMPSHIRE COUNTY COUNCIL
County Adoption Services
Glenhouse
Glen Road
Swanwick
SOUTHAMPTON
SO31 7HD
Tel: 01489 587543
and
County Adoption Team
Hamble Cottage, Glen Road
Swanwick
SOUTHAMPTON
SO31 7HD
Tel: 01489 587000

HARINGEY, LONDON BOROUGH OF
Adoption Team
40 Cumberland Road
Wood Green
LONDON
N22 7SG
Tel: 020 8489 3774
www.haringey.gov.uk

HARROW, LONDON BOROUGH OF
Family Placement Service
Social Services Department
429 – 433 Pinner Road
NORTH HARROW
HA1 4HN
Tel: 020 8863 5544
www.harrow.gov.uk

HAVERING, LONDON BOROUGH OF
Family Placement Team
Midland House
109 – 113 Victoria Road
ROMFORD
Essex
RM1 2LX
Tel: 01708 434543
www.havering.gov.uk

HERTFORDSHIRE COUNTY COUNCIL
Adoption Team (East Herts)
16 Warren Park Road
HERTFORD
Hertfordshire
SG14 3JD
www.hertsdirect.org
and
Adoption Team (West Herts)
Old Parkway School
Parkway
WELWYN GARDEN CITY

Hertfordshire
AL8 6JD
Tel: 01707 897654
www.hertsdirect.org

HILLINGDON, LONDON BOROUGH OF
Fostering and Adoption Service
Civic Centre
4S/06 High Street
OXBRIDGE
UB8 1UW
Tel: 01895 277845
www.hillingdon.gov.uk

HOUNSLOW, LONDON BOROUGH OF
Family Placement Section
The Civic Centre
Lampton Road
HOUNSLOW
Middlesex
TW3 4DN
Tel: 020 8583 3437
Email: adoptioninfo.sshp@
hounslow.gov.uk or
adoption.duty@hounslow.gov.uk
www.hounslow.gov.uk

ISLE OF WIGHT COUNCIL
Family Placement Team
Adoption Service
St James's Centre
4 – 5 St James's Street
NEWPORT
Isle of Wight
PO30 5HE
Tel: 01983 814370
www.iwight.com

ISLINGTON, LONDON BOROUGH OF
The Adoption Service
11 – 12 Highbury Crescent

LONDON
N5 1RN
Tel: 020 7527 4400
www.islington.gov.uk/adoption

JERSEY, STATES OF
Children's Service
Maison Le Pape
The Parade, St Helier
JERSEY
JE2 3PU
Tel: 01534 623500

**KENSINGTON & CHELSEA,
ROYAL BOROUGH OF**
Family Placement Unit
The Adoption Team
Westway Aid and Information Centre
140 Ladbroke Grove
North Kensington
LONDON
W10 5ND
Tel: 020 7598 4444
Email: ss.c&f.familyplacement
@rbkc.gov.uk
www.rbkc.gov.uk

KENT COUNTY COUNCIL
West Kent Adoption Team
17 Kings Hill Avenue
Kings Hill
WEST MALLING
Kent
ME19 4UL
Tel: 01732 525000
www.kentadoption.com
and
East Kent Adoption Team
Kroner House
Eurogate Business Park
ASHFORD
Kent
TN24 8XU

Tel: 01233 898632
www.kentadoption.com

**KINGSTON UPON THAMES,
ROYAL BOROUGH OF**
Learning and Children Services
Family Placement Team
Room 205, Guildhall 1
High Street
KINGSTON UPON THAMES
Surrey
KT1 1EU
Tel: 020 8547 6042
www.kingston.gov.uk

**LAMBETH, LONDON BOROUGH
OF**
Adoption Team
3rd Floor, Hopton House
243A Streatham High Street
LONDON
SW16 6EY
Tel: 020 7926 8503

**LEWISHAM, LONDON BOROUGH
OF**
Social Services Department
Adoption Team
St Paul's House
125 Deptford High Street
LONDON
SE8 4NS
Tel: 020 8314 8639/6000
www.lewisham.gov.uk

LUTON COUNCIL
Social Services Department
Adoption Team
Unity House, 111 Stuart Street
LUTON
LU1 5NP
Tel: 01582 547568
Email: adoptions@luton.gov.uk
www.luton.gov.uk

MEDWAY COUNCIL
Children's Services
Homefinding Team
Compass Centre
Chatham Maritime
CHATHAM
ME4 4YH
Tel: 01634 331113
www.medway.gov.uk

MERTON, LONDON BOROUGH OF
Adoption and Permanency Team
Worsfold House, Church Road
MITCHAM
Surrey
CR4 3FA
Tel: 020 8545 4277/4289
www.merton.gov.uk/adoptionandfostering

MILTON KEYNES COUNCIL
Learning and Development Directorate
Children's Services
Saxon Court
502 Avebury Boulevard
MILTON KEYNES
MK9 3HS
Tel: 01908 253404
www.mkweb.co.uk

NEWHAM, LONDON BOROUGH OF
The Adoption Team
16 Wordsworth Avenue
Manor Park
LONDON
E12 6SU
Tel: 0800 783 6388
www.newham.gov.uk

NORFOLK COUNTY COUNCIL
Adoption and Family Finding Unit
3 Unthank Road
NORWICH
NR2 2PA

Tel: 01603 617796
www.norfolk.gov.uk

NORTH SOMERSET DISTRICT COUNCIL
Adoption and Fostering Team
Children and Young People's Services
PO Box 195
Town Hall
WESTON-SUPER-MARE
BS23 1UF
Tel: 01275 888236
www.n-somerset.gov.uk

OXFORDSHIRE COUNTY COUNCIL
Oxford Social and Health Care
Family Placement Team
The City Office
134B Cowley Road
OXFORD
OX4 1JH
Tel: 01865 815347 or 815237
www.oxfordshire.gov.uk

PETERBOROUGH CITY COUNCIL
Adoption and Fostering Unit
3rd Floor, Midgate House
Midgate
PETERBOROUGH
PE1 1TN
Tel: 01733 746179
www.peterborough.gov.uk

PLYMOUTH CITY COUNCIL
The Adoption Team
Midland House
City of Plymouth
PLYMOUTH
PL1 2AA
Tel: 01752 306800
www.plymouth.gov.uk/adoption

POOLE BOROUGH COUNCIL
Adoption and Fostering Team
Children and Families Services
14A Commercial Road
Parkstone
POOLE
BH14 OJW
Tel: 01202 714711
www.poole.gov.uk

PORTSMOUTH CITY COUNCIL
Health, Housing and Social Care
Adoption Section
1st Floor, Civic Offices
Guildhall Square
PORTSMOUTH
PO1 2EP
Tel: 023 9284 1626
www.portsmouth.gov.uk

READING BOROUGH COUNCIL
Adoption Team
PO Box 2624
READING
Berkshire
RG1 7WB
Tel: 0118 955 3740
www.reading.gov.uk

**REDBRIDGE, LONDON BOROUGH
OF**
Fostering and Adoption Service
Station Road
BARKINGSIDE
Essex
IG6 1NB
Tel: 020 8708 7528
www.redbridgekids.org.uk

**RICHMOND UPON THAMES,
LONDON BOROUGH OF**
Fostering and Adoption Services
Services for Children and Families
42 York Street

TWICKENHAM
TW1 3BW
Tel: 020 8891 7754
www.richmond.gov.uk

SLOUGH BOROUGH COUNCIL
Family Placement Service
Room GE06, Town Hall
Bath Road
SLOUGH
SL1 3UQ
or
Freepost
FCE 8944
SLOUGH
SL1 3BR
Tel: 01753 690960 or 0800 073 0291
Email: familyplacement@slough.gov.uk
www.slough.gov.uk

SOMERSET COUNTY COUNCIL
Central Adoption Team
Children's Social Care
A Block
County Hall
TAUNTON
Somerset
TA1 4DY
Tel: 01823 355130

**SOUTH GLOUCESTERSHIRE
COUNCIL**
Family Placement Team
Heath Resource Centre
2A Newton Road
Cadbury Heath
BRISTOL
BS30 8EZ
Tel: 01454 866088
www.southglos.gov.uk

SOUTHAMPTON CITY COUNCIL
Adoption Services
Cedar Road Resource Centre

30A Cedar Road
SOUTHAMPTON
Hampshire
SO14 6HL
Tel: 023 8044 6450
www.southampton.gov.uk

SOUTHEND COUNCIL
Family Finders
Adoption and Fostering
283 London Road
WESTCLIFFE-ON-SEA
Essex
SS0 7ZX
Tel: 01702 354366 or 534090
www.southend.gov.uk

**SOUTHWARK, LONDON
BOROUGH OF**
Adoption and Fostering Unit
47B East Dulwich Road
LONDON
SE22 9BZ
Tel: 020 7525 4489/4863
www.southwark.gov.uk

SUFFOLK COUNTY COUNCIL
Suffolk Adoption Agency
Principal's House
Stoke Road
THORNDON
Suffolk
IP23 7JG
Tel: 01379 672750
or
St Edmund House
Rope Walk
IPSWICH
IP4 1LZ
Tel: 01473 583435
www.suffolkadoption.com

SURREY COUNTY COUNCIL
Adoption and Permanency Service
Belair House

Chertsey Boulevard
Hanworth Lane
CHERTSEY
Surrey
KT16 9JX
Tel: 01932 794340
Email: adoption@surreycc.gov.uk
www.surreycc.gov.uk

SUTTON, LONDON BOROUGH OF
Adoption and Fostering Team
The Lodge
Honeywood Walk
CARSHALTON
Surrey
SM5 3NX
Tel: 020 8770 4477
www.sutton.gov.uk

SWINDON BOROUGH COUNCIL
Children's Services
Family Placement Team
Hut 8
Civic Offices
Euclid Street
SWINDON
SN1 2JH
Tel: 01793 465700
Email: familyplacement@swindon.gov.uk
www.swindon.gov.uk

THURROCK COUNCIL
Children, Education and Families
Fostering and Adoption Team
PO Box 140
Civic Offices
New Road
GRAYS
Essex
RM17 6TJ
Tel: 01375 652617
www.thurrock.gov.uk

TORBAY COUNCIL
Torbay Adoption Team

Parkfield House
38 Esplanade Road
PAIGNTON
Devon
TQ3 2NH
Tel: 01803 402752
Email: adoption.team@torbay.gov.uk
www.torbay.gov.uk

**TOWER HAMLETS, LONDON
BOROUGH OF**
Family Placement Service
117 Poplar High Street
Poplar
LONDON
E14 0AE
Tel: 020 7364 5000/5390
www.fosteringandadoption.co.uk

**WALTHAM FOREST, LONDON
BOROUGH OF**
Fostering and Adoption Service
1C The Drive
Walthamstow
LONDON
E17 3BN
Tel: 020 8496 3000/1588
www.lbwf.gov.uk

**WANDSWORTH, LONDON
BOROUGH OF**
Adoption and Fostering Unit
Welbeck House
4th floor
43 – 51 Wandsworth High Street
LONDON
SW18 2PU
Tel: 020 8871 7261
Email: adoptionandfostering@
wandsworth.gov.uk
www.wandsworth.gov.uk

WEST BERKSHIRE COUNCIL
Family Placement Team
Avonbank House

West Street
Newbury
NEWBURY
RG14 1BZ
Tel: 01635 503155
www.westberks.gov.uk

WEST SUSSEX COUNTY COUNCIL
The Adoption Team
Harwood House
Kings Road
HORSHAM
RH13 5PR
Tel: 01403 246416
Email: adoption.team@
westsussex.gov.uk
www.westsussex.gov.uk

CITY OF WESTMINSTER
Family Placements Service
1st Floor, 4 Frampton Street
LONDON
NW8 8LF
Tel: 020 7641 4080
www.westminster.gov.uk

WILTSHIRE COUNTY COUNCIL
(North Wiltshire and Kenet District)
Children's Resource Centre
357 Hungerdown Lane
CHIPPENHAM
Wiltshire
SN14 0UY
Tel: 01249 444321 or 0800 169 6321
www.wiltshire.gov.uk
and
(West Wiltshire)
Trowbridge Resource Centre
53 Rutland Crescent
TROWBRIDGE
Wiltshire
BA14 0NY
Tel: 01225 752198
and

(Salisbury)
Salisbury Office
Riverside Children's Resource Centre
29 Churchfields Road
SALISBURY
Wiltshire
SP2 7NH
Tel: 01722 333552

WINDSOR & MAIDENHEAD, ROYAL BOROUGH OF
Social Services
Fostering, Adoption and Respite Services
4 Marlow Road
MAIDENHEAD
Berkshire
SL6 7YR
Tel: 01628 683201
Email: adoption_fostering@
rbwm.gov.uk
www.rbwm.gov.uk

WOKINGHAM DISTRICT COUNCIL
Children's Services
The Family Placement Team
Lytham Court
Lytham Road
WOODLEY
RG5 3PQ
Tel: 0118 944 5468
Email:
familyplacement@wokingham.gov.uk
www.wokingham.gov.uk

VOLUNTARY AGENCIES

ADOLESCENT AND CHILDREN'S TRUST (TACT)
Head Office
The Courtyard
303 Hither Green Lane

LONDON
SE13 6TJ
Tel: 020 8695 8111
Email: adoption@tactfostercare.org.uk
www.tactfostercare.org.uk

ADOPT ANGLIA PROJECT
9 Petersfield
CAMBRIDGE
CB1 1BB
Tel: 01223 357397
www.koram.org.uk

BARNARDO'S JIGSAW PROJECT
12 Church Hill
Walthamstow
LONDON
E17 3AG
Tel: 020 8521 0033

BARNARDO'S NEW FAMILIES PROJECT
54 Head Street
COLCHESTER
Essex
CO1 1PB
Tel: 01206 562438

CATHOLIC CHILDREN'S SOCIETY (ARUNDEL & BRIGHTON, PORTSMOUTH & BRIGHTON)
49 Russell Hill Road
PURLEY
Surrey
CR8 2XB
Tel: 020 8668 2181
Email: info@cathchild.org
www.cathchild.org.uk

CATHOLIC CHILDREN'S SOCIETY (DIOCESE OF CLIFTON)
162 Pennywell Road
Eastern
BRISTOL

BS5 0TX
Tel: 0845 122 0077
Email: info@ccsadoption.org
www.ccsadoption.org

CATHOLIC CHILDREN'S SOCIETY (FAMILY MAKERS GRAVESEND)

Family Finders
28 Leith Park Road
GRAVESEND
DA12 1LW
Tel: 01474 352521

CATHOLIC CHILDREN'S SOCIETY (LITTLEHAMPTON)

4 St Catherine's Road
LITTLEHAMPTON
West Sussex
BN17 5HS
Tel: 01903 715317

CATHOLIC CHILDREN'S SOCIETY(WESTMINSTER)

73 St Charles's Square
LONDON
W10 6EJ
Tel: 020 8969 5305
Email: info@cathchild.org.uk
www.cathchild.org.uk

CHILDLINK ADOPTION SOCIETY

10 Lion Yard
Tremadoc Road
LONDON
SW4 7NQ
Tel: 020 7501 1700
www.adoptchildlink.org.uk

CORAM FAMILY

49 Mecklenburgh Square
LONDON
WC1N 2QA
Tel: 020 7520 0300
Email: reception@coram.org.uk
www.coram.org.uk

FAMILIES FOR CHILDREN TRUST

Southgate Court
Buckfast
BUCKFASTLEIGH
Devon
TQ11 0EE
Tel: 01364 645480
www.familiesforchildren.org.uk

INDEPENDENT ADOPTION SERVICE

121 – 123 Camberwell Road
LONDON
SE5 0HB
Tel: 020 7703 1088
Email: admin@i-a-s.org.uk
www.independentadoptionservice.org.uk

NCH

Adoption and Fostercare
(NCH Southwest)
Weirhouse
93 Whitby Road
St Phillips
BRISTOL
BS4 4AR
Tel: 0117 300 5360

NCH

Adoption NCH South East
158 Crawley Road
Roffey
HORSHAM
West Sussex
RH12 4EU
Tel: 01403 225916

NCH

London Black Families Adoption
Project
12A Hackford Walk
Hackford Road
LONDON
SW9 0ZT
Tel: 020 7582 3687

**NORWOOD JEWISH ADOPTION
SOCIETY**
Broadway House
80 – 82 The Broadway
STANMORE
Middlesex
HA7 4HB
Tel: 020 8954 4555
www.norwood.org.uk

**PARENTS AND CHILDREN
TOGETHER (PACT)**
7 Southern Court
South Street
READING
Berkshire
RG1 4QS
Tel: 0118 938 7600
email: info@pactcharity.org
www.pactcharity.org

PARENTS FOR CHILDREN
Club Union House
253 – 254 Upper Street
Islington

LONDON
N1 1RY
Tel: 020 7288 4320
Email: info@parentsforchildren.org.uk

**SOLDIERS' SAILORS' AIRMENS'
FAMILIES ASSOCIATION (SSAFA)
– FORCES HELP**
19 Queen Elizabeth Street
LONDON
SE1 2LP
Tel: 020 7403 8783
Email: info@ssafa.org.uk
www.ssafa.org.uk

**ST FRANCIS' CHILDREN'S
SOCIETY**
Collis House
48 Newport Road
Woolstone
MILTON KEYNES
MK15 0AA
Tel: 01908 572700
Email: enquiries@sfcs.org.uk
www.sfcs.org.uk

CYMRU

BAAF CYMRU
7 Cleeve House
Lambourne Crescent
CARDIFF
CF14 5GJ
Tel: 029 2076 1155
Email: cymru@baaf.org.uk

and at

19 Bedford Street
RHYL
Denbighshire
LL18 1SY
Tel: 01745 336336
Email: cymru.rhyl@baaf.org.uk

and at

Unit 2, Hendy Industrial Estate
Hendy
SWANSEA
SA4 0XP
Tel: 01792 885129

Email: cymru.swansea
@baaf.org.uk

**North Wales Adoption
Consortium**
Address as BAAF Rhyl
Tel: 01745 345012
Email: nwac@baaf.org.uk

**South Wales Adoption
Consortium**
Address as BAAF Cardiff
Tel: 029 2076 4849

LOCAL AUTHORITY AGENCIES

**ANGLESEY COUNTY COUNCIL,
ISLE OF**
Social Services Department
County Offices
LLANGEFNI
LL77 7TW
Tel: 01248 752733
www.anglesey.gov.uk

**BLAENAU GWENT COUNTY
BOROUGH COUNCIL**
Ebbw Vale Social Services
7 Bridge Street
EBBW VALE
Blaenau
Gwent
NP23 6EY
Tel: 01495 350555

**BRIDGEND COUNTY BOROUGH
COUNCIL**
Personal Services Directorate
Adoption Team

Sunnyside
BRIDGEND
CF31 4AR
Tel: 01656 642200
www.bridgend.gov.uk

CAERPHILLY COUNTY BOROUGH COUNCIL
Social Services Department
Adoption Team
Avenue House
2 King Edward Avenue
CAERPHILLY
CF83 1HE
Tel: 0800 587 5664
www.caerphilly.gov.uk

CARDIFF COUNCIL
Children's Services
Trowbridge Centre
Greenway Road
Rumney
CARDIFF
CF3 1QS
Tel: 029 2077 4600
www.cardiff.gov.uk

CARMARTHENSHIRE COUNTY COUNCIL
Social Services Department
3 Spilman Street
CARMARTHEN
SA31 1LE
Tel: 01554 742380
www.carmarthenshire.gov.uk

CEREDIGION COUNTY COUNCIL
Social Services Department
Looked After Children's Service
Headquarters
Min Aeron, Vicarage Hill
Aberaeron
CEREDIGION
SA46 0DY

Tel: 01545 572630/574000
www.ceredigion.gov.uk

CONWY COUNTY BOROUGH COUNCIL
Fostering and Adoption Agency
1 – 2 Chapel Street
LLANDUDNO
Conwy
LL30 2SY
Tel: 01492 878 914
www.conwy.gov.uk

DENBIGHSHIRE COUNTY COUNCIL
Social Services Department
Cefndy Children's Resource Centre
Cefndy Road
RHYL
Denbighshire
LL18 2HG
Tel: 01824 712200
www.denbighshire.gov.uk

FLINTSHIRE COUNTY COUNCIL
Children's Services
County Offices
Wepre Drive
CONNAH'S QUAY
Deeside
Flintshire
CH5 4HB
Tel: 01352 701000
Email: adoption@flintshire.gov.uk
www.flintshire.gov.uk

GWYNEDD COUNCIL
Fostering and Adoption Department
Penrallt
CAERNARFON
Gwynedd
LL55 1BN
Tel: 01286 682660
www.gwynedd.gov.uk

ISLE OF ANGLESEY COUNTY COUNCIL
See ANGLESEY COUNTY COUNCIL

MERTHYR TYDFIL COUNTY BOROUGH COUNCIL
The Adoption Team
Merthyr Tydfil Integrated Children's Services
Tag Fechan Buildings
Castle Street
MERTHYR TYDFIL
CF47 8BG
Tel: 01685 724555
www.merthyr.gov.uk

MONMOUTHSHIRE COUNTY COUNCIL
Family Placements
Social and Housing Services
Newbridge House
Baker Street
ABERGAVENNY
Monmouthshire
NP7 5HU
Tel: 01873 735900
www.monmouthshire.gov.uk

NEATH PORT TALBOT COUNTY BOROUGH COUNCIL
The Laurels
87 Lewis Road
NEATH
SA11 1DJ
Tel: 01639 765400
www.neath-porttalbot.gov.uk

NEWPORT CITY COUNCIL
Children and Family Services
The Adoption Team
Corn Exchange, High Street
NEWPORT
NP20 1RN
Tel: 01633 235453

Email: fosteringandadoption@
newport.gov.uk
www.newport.gov.uk

PEMBROKESHIRE COUNTY COUCIL
Family Placement Team
The Elms
Golden Hill Road
PEMBROKE
SA71 4QB
Tel: 01646 683747
www.pembrokeshire.gov.uk

POWYS COUNTY COUNCIL
Social Services Department
Children's Services
The Annex, Watton Mount
The Watton
BRECON
Powys
LD3 7BB
Tel: 01874 624298
www.powys.gov.uk

RHONDDA CYNON TAF COUNTY BOROUGH COUNCIL
Looked After Children's Services and
Education Services
Maes-y-Coed
Lanelay Terrace
Pontypridd
RHONDDA CYNON TAF
CF37 1ER
Tel: 01443 490710
www.rhondda-cynon-taff.gov.uk

SWANSEA, CITY AND COUNTY OF
Adoption Section
The Family Placement Team
Cockett House
Cockett Road
Cockett

SWANSEA
SA2 0FJ
Tel: 01792 522900
www.swansea.gov.uk

TORFAEN COUNTY BOROUGH COUNCIL
Social Services Department
The Family Placement Team
County Hall
CWMBRAN
Torfaen
NP44 2WN
Tel: 01633 648540
www.torfaen.gov.uk

VALE OF GLAMORGAN COUNCIL
Fostering and Adoption Resource Centre
14 Albert Crescent
PENARTH
CF64 1DA
Tel: 029 2035 0950
www.valeofglamorgan.gov.uk

WREXHAM COUNTY BOROUGH COUNCIL
Personal Services Department
3 – 9 Grosvenor Road
WREXHAM
LL11 1DB
Tel: 01978 291422 or 267202
www.wrexham.gov.uk

VOLUNTARY AGENCIES

ADOLESCENT AND CHILDREN'S TRUST (TACT)
TACT Cymru
20 Victoria Gardens
NEATH
South Wales
SA11 3BH
Tel: 01639 622320
Email: adoption@tactfostercare.org.uk
www.tactfostercare.org.uk

BARNARDO'S
Derwen Family Placement Services
3 Raleigh Walk
Brigantine Place
CARDIFF
CF10 4LN
Tel: 029 2043 6200
Email: cymru.derwen@barnardos.org.uk
www.barnardos.org.uk

ST. DAVID'S CHILDREN'S SOCIETY
Bishop Brown House, Durham Street
Grangetown
CARDIFF
CF11 6PB
Tel: 029 2066 7007
Email: stdavidscf@aol.com

BAAF SCOTLAND
40 Shandwick Place
EDINBURGH
EH2 4RT
Tel: 0131 220 4749
Email: scotland@baaf.org.uk

West of Scotland Family Placement Consortium
Address as above
Tel: 0131 226 9290
Email: west.scotland@ baaf.org.uk

North East Scotland Consortium
Address as above
Tel: 0131 226 9299

LOCAL AUTHORITY AGENCIES

ABERDEEN CITY COUNCIL
Neighbourhood Services Social Work
Adoption and Fostering Team
77/79 King Street
ABERDEEN
AB24 5AB
Tel: 01224 793830
www.aberdeencity.gov.uk

ABERDEENSHIRE COUNCIL
Family Placement Team
93 High Street
INVERURIE
AB51 3AB
Tel: 01467 625555
Email: adoption@aberdeenshire.gov.uk
www.aberdeenshire.gov.uk

ANGUS COUNCIL
Family Placement Team
Academy Lane
ARBROATH
DD11 1EJ
Tel: 01241 435680/878585
Email: russellc@angus.gov.uk
www.angus.gov.uk

ARGYLL & BUTE COUNCIL
Community Services
Children and Families
Kilmory
LOCHGILPHEAD
PA31 8RT
Tel: 01546 602177
www.argyll-bute.gov.uk

CLACKMANNANSHIRE COUNCIL
Social Work Department
Childcare Services,
Alloa Centre, 8 Hillcrest Drive
ALLOA
FK10 1SB
Tel: 01259 225000
www.clacks.gov.uk

**COMHAIRLE NAN EILEAN SIAR
(WESTERN ISLES COUNCIL)**
Social Work Department
Council Offices
Rathad Shanndabhaig (Sandwick Road)
STEORNABHAGH (STORNOWAY)
Isle of Lewis
HS1 2BW
Tel: 01851 703773
Email: imacaulay@cne-siar.gov.uk
www.cne-siar.gov.uk

**DUMFRIES & GALLOWAY
COUNCIL**
Fostering and Adoption Team
The Portacabins
27 Moffat Road
DUMFRIES
DG1 1NB
Tel: 01387 260677
www.dumgal.gov.uk

DUNDEE CITY COUNCIL
Family Placement Team
The Social Work Offices
Jack Martin Way
DUNDEE
DD4 9FF
Tel: 01382 436000
www.dundeecity.gov.uk

EAST AYRSHIRE COUNCIL
Social Work Department
Fostering and Adoption Team
Civic Centre, John Dickie Street
KILMARNOCK

KA1 1BY
Tel: 01563 576905
www.east-ayrshire.gov.uk

**EAST DUNBARTONSHIRE
COUNCIL**
Social Work Department
William Patrick Library
2 – 4 West High Street
Kirkintilloch
GLASGOW
G66 1AD
Tel: 0141 775 9000
www.eastdunbarton.gov.uk

EAST LOTHIAN COUNCIL
Children and Families Community
Services Department
Sinclair McGill Buildings
6 – 8 Lodge Street
HADDINGTON
EH41 3DX
Tel: 01620 826600

EAST RENFREWSHIRE COUNCIL
Social Work Department
Lygates House, 224 – 226 Ayr Road
NEWTON MEARNS
East Renfrewshire
G77 6FR
Tel: 0141 577 3367
www.eastrenfrewshire.gov.uk

CITY OF EDINBURGH COUNCIL
Children and Families Resource Team
Springwell House, 1 Gorgie Road
EDINBURGH
EH11 2LA
Tel: 0131 313 6774
www.edinburgh.gov.uk

FALKIRK COUNCIL
Social Work Services
Adoption and Fostering Team
Brockville, Hope Street

FALKIRK
FK1 5RW
Tel: 01324 506400
www.falkirk.gov.uk

FIFE COUNCIL
Adoption and Fostering Team
Rosyth Social Work Office
Park Road
ROSYTH
Fife
KY11 2JL
Tel: 01383 313345
www.fife.gov.uk

GLASGOW CITY COUNCIL
Families for Children
Centenary House, 100 Morrison Street
GLASGOW
G5 8LN
Tel: 0141 420 5555
Email: families.children@glasgow.gov.uk
www.glasgow.gov.uk

HIGHLAND COUNCIL
Family Resource Centre
Limetree Avenue
INVERNESS
IV3 5RH
Tel: 01463 234120
www.highland.gov.uk

INVERCLYDE COUNCIL
Social Work
Children and Families Section
195 Dalrymple Street
GREENOCK
PA15 1LD
Tel: 01475 714038
www.inverclyde.gov.uk

MIDLOTHIAN COUNCIL
11 St Andrews Street
DALKEITH
Midlothian

EH22 1AL
Tel: 0131 271 3860
www.midlothian.gov.uk

MORAY COUNCIL
Fostering and Adoption Team
6 Moss Street
ELGIN
Moray
IV30 1LU
Tel: 01343 563568
www.moray.org

NORTH AYRSHIRE COUNCIL
The Family Placement Team
17 – 23 Byres Road
KILWINNING
KA13 6JY
Tel: 01294 559820
www.north-ayrshire.gov.uk

NORTH LANARKSHIRE COUNCIL
Fostering and Adoption Team
Social Work Department
Scott House, 73/77 Merry Street
MOTHERWELL
ML1 1JE
Tel: 01698 332100
Email: northrecservices@
northlan.gov.uk
www.northlan.gov.uk

ORKNEY ISLANDS COUNCIL
Children and Families Team
Council Offices
School Place
KIRKWELL
KW15 1NY
Tel: 01856 873535

PERTH & KINROSS COUNCIL
Education and Children's Services
Colonsay Resource Centre
37 – 39 Colonsay Street
North Muirton

PERTH
PH1 3TU
Tel: 01738 626940
www.pkc.gov.uk

RENFREWSHIRE COUNCIL
Social Work Department
North Building, 4th Floor, Cotton Street
PAISLEY
PA1 1TZ
Tel: 0141 842 5158
www.renfrewshire.gov.uk

SCOTTISH BORDERS COUNCIL
Family Placement Team
Children's Services
11 Market Street
GALASHIELS
TD1 3AD
Tel: 01896 757230
Email: mablackie@
scotborders.gsx.gov.uk
www.scotborders.gov.uk

SHETLAND ISLANDS COUNCIL
Social Work Department
91 – 93 St Olaf Street
LERWICK
Shetland
ZE1 0ES
Tel: 01595 744400
www.sic.shetland.gov.uk

SOUTH AYRSHIRE COUNCIL
Social Work Department
Whitlets Area Centre
Whitlets Road
AYR
Tel: 01292 267675
www.south-ayrshire.gov.uk

SOUTH LANARKSHIRE COUNCIL
Social Work Department
Adoption and Fostering
4th Floor

Brandongate
1 Leachlee Road
HAMILTON
ML3 0XB
Tel: 01698 455400
www.southlanarkshire.gov.uk

STIRLING COUNCIL
Social Work Department
Drummond House, Wellgreen Place
STIRLING
FK8 2EG
Tel: 0845 277 7000 or 01786 471177
www.stirling.gov.uk

**WEST DUNBARTONSHIRE
COUNCIL**
Social Work Department
7 Bruce Street
CLYDEBANK
G81 1DT
Tel: 0141 951 6198
www.west_dunbarton.gov.uk

WEST LOTHIAN COUNCIL
Children and Families Resources Team
Lomond House
Beveridge Square
LIVINGSTON
EH54 6QF
Tel: 01506 775959
www.resources.ukfamily.com or
www.westlothian.gov.uk

WESTERN ISLES COUNCIL
See COMHAIRLE NAN EILEAN SIAR

VOLUNTARY AGENCIES

BARNARDO'S FAMILY PLACEMENT SERVICES
6 Torphichen Street
EDINBURGH
EH3 8JQ
Tel: 0131 228 41212
Email: fpsscotland@barnardos.org.uk
www.barnardos.org.uk

FAMILY CARE
21 Castle Street
EDINBURGH
EH2 3DN
Tel: 0131 225 6441
Email: mail@birthlink.org.uk
www.birthlink.org.uk

ST ANDREW'S CHILDREN'S SOCIETY
7 John's Place
Leith
EDINBURGH
EH6 7EL

Tel: 0131 454 3370
Email: info@standrews-children.org.uk
www.standrews-children.org.uk

ST MARGARET'S CHILDREN & FAMILY CARE SOCIETY
274 Bath Street
GLASGOW
G2 4JR
Tel: 0141 332 8371
Email: info@stmargarets-cafcs.org.uk
www.stmargarets-cafcs.org.uk

SCOTTISH ADOPTION ASSOCIATION
161 Constitution Street
Leith
EDINBURGH
EH6 7DF
Tel: 0131 553 5060
Email: info@scottishadoption.org
www.scottishadoption.org

NORTHERN IRELAND

BAAF expects to open an office in Northern Ireland from April 2006 – check www.baaf.org.uk for update. Until that time, enquiries should be directed to:
BAAF Southern Region
Saffron House
6 – 10 Kirby Street
LONDON
EC1N 8TS
Tel: 020 7421 2670/71

Note: Adoption and Fostering Units are located in Health and Social Services Trusts which are divided into four regional Boards.

EHSSB COMMUNITY TRUSTS

DOWN & LISBURN HEALTH & SOCIAL SERVICES TRUST
Warren Resource Centre
61 Woodland Park
LISBURN
BT28 1LQ
Tel: 028 9260 7528
www.dlt.n-i.nhs.uk

ULSTER COMMUNITY & HOSPITALS TRUST
Family Placement Team
Dunlop Units 57 and 58
4 Balloo Drive
BANGOR
County Down
BT19 7QY
Tel: 028 9127 0672

NORTH & WEST BELFAST HEALTH AND SOCIAL SERVICES TRUST
Glendinning House, 6 Murray Street
BELFAST
BT1 6DP
Tel: 028 9024 5000
Email: fosteringandadoption@ nwb.n-i.nhs.uk
www.nwb.n-i.nhs.uk

SOUTH & EAST BELFAST HEALTH & SOCIAL SERVICES TRUST
33 Wellington Park
BELFAST
BT9 6DL
Tel: 028 9020 4500
www.sebt.n-i.nhs.uk

NHSSB COMMUNITY TRUSTS

HOMEFIRST SOCIAL SERVICES TRUST
Audley Terrace
27 Ballymoney Road
BALLYMENA
County Antrim
BT43 5BS
Tel: 028 2564 1207
www.homefirst.n-i.nhs.uk

CAUSEWAY HEALTH & SOCIAL SERVICES TRUST
Family Placement Team
Riverside House, 28 Port Stewart Road
COLERAINE
BT52 1RN
Tel: 028 7035 8158

WHSSB COMMUNITY TRUSTS

FOYLE HEALTH & SOCIAL SERVICES TRUST
Family and Childcare Team
Rassdowney House
Glendermott Road
Waterside
DERRY
BT47 6BG
Tel: 028 7126 6111
www.foyletrust.n-i.nhs.uk

SPERRIN & LAKELAND HEALTH & SOCIAL SERVICES TRUST
The Family Placement Team
Community Services Department
Tyrone and Fermanagh Hospital
OMAGH
BT79 0NS
Tel: 028 8283 5114
www.sperrin-lakeland.org

SHSSB COMMUNITY TRUSTS

ARMAGH & DUNGANNON HEALTH & SOCIAL SERVICES TRUST
Family Placement Service
The Bungalow, Drumglass Lodge
20 Coalisland Road
DUNGANNON
BT71 6LA
Tel: 028 8775 2033
www.adhsst.n-i.nhs.uk

CRAIGAVON & BANBRIDGE COMMUNITY HEALTH & SOCIAL SERVICES TRUST
Family Placement Service
Borombra Lodge
2 Old Lurgan Road
PORTADOWN
BT63 5SG
Tel: 028 3833 7181
www.cbct.n-i.nhs.uk

NEWRY & MOURNE HEALTH & SOCIAL SERVICES TRUST
Family Placement Team
Dromalane House
Dromalane Road
NEWRY
BT35 8AP
Tel: 028 3082 5000
Email: familyplacement@dhh.n-i.nhs.uk
www.dhh.n-i.nhs.uk

VOLUNTARY AGENCIES

CHURCH OF IRELAND ADOPTION SOCIETY
Church of Ireland House
61 – 67 Donegall Street
BELFAST
BT1 2QH
Tel: 028 9023 3885
Email: bsr@ireland.anglican.org
www.cofiadopt.org.uk

FAMILY CARE SOCIETY (NORTHERN IRELAND)
511 Ormeau Road
BELFAST
BT7 3GS
Tel: 028 9069 1133
www.family-care-society.org

BAAF and other useful organisations

British Association for Adoption and Fostering (BAAF)

BAAF is the leading UK-wide organisation for all those working in the adoption, fostering and childcare fields. BAAF's work includes giving advice and information to members of the public on aspects of adoption, fostering and childcare issues; publishing a wide range of books, training packs and leaflets as well as a quarterly journal on adoption, fostering and childcare issues; providing training and consultancy services to social workers and other professionals to help them improve the quality of medical, legal and social work services to children and families; giving evidence to government committees on subjects concerning children and families; responding to consultative documents on changes in legislation and regulations affecting children in or at risk of coming into care; and helping to find new families for children through *Be My Parent*.

Almost all local authority and voluntary adoption agencies are members of BAAF. You can join BAAF as an individual member; contact the Membership Officer for details of benefits and fees. Telephone 020 7421 2635 or visit www.baaf.org.uk for more information. BAAF is a registered charity.

Be My Parent

Every month, between 300 and 400 children waiting for new permanent families are featured in *Be My Parent*, the UK-wide family-finding newspaper published by BAAF. Subscribers to *Be My Parent* include approved adopters, those waiting to be approved and those who have only just begun to think about adopting or permanently fostering. Children of all ages and with a wide range of needs from all over the country are featured, and therefore *Be*

My Parent seeks as wide a readership as possible. Many hundreds of families (married couples and single people) have adopted after first having seen their child's photograph and read their profile in *Be My Parent*. It is easy to subscribe and have the newspaper sent directly to you – just telephone the number below. If you see children in *Be My Parent* whom you would like to become part of your family, one telephone call to our staff will begin the process that could lead to you becoming approved to adopt that child.

Be My Parent is at

BAAF
Saffron House
6 – 10 Kirby Street
London EC1N 8TS
Tel: 020 7421 2666
Email: bmp@baaf.org.uk

| Scottish Resource Network

The Scottish Resource Network is a child placement service run by BAAF in Scotland. The West of Scotland and North East Scotland Consortia facilitate the placement of children across local authority boundaries in Scotland. Information about the Scottish Resource Network and the West of Scotland and North East Scotland Consortia can be obtained from BAAF Scotland (see below).

| BAAF Offices

More information about BAAF can be obtained from:

Head Office
Saffron House
6 – 10 Kirby Stree
London EC1N 8TS
Tel: 020 7421 2600
Fax: 020 7421 2601
Email: mail@baaf.org.uk

BAAF Scotland
40 Shandwick Place
Edinburgh EH2 4RT
Tel: 0131 220 4749
Fax: 0131 226 3778
Email: scotland@baaf.org.uk

BAAF Cymru
7 Cleeve House
Lambourne Crescent
Cardiff CF14 5GP
Tel: 029 2076 1155
Fax: 029 2074 7934
Email: cymru@baaf.org.uk

A full list of BAAF's offices is provided in Chapter 9.

Adoption Register for England and Wales

The Adoption Register is a database of waiting approved adopters
and children for whom adoption is the plan. It has been fully
operational since April 2002 and has been run by BAAF on
behalf of the Department for Education and Skills since
December 2004. Its purpose is to increase the opportunities of
finding a family for children waiting for adoption. Only adoption
agencies in England and Wales can refer adopters and children to
the Register.

The Adoption Register has two main elements. Firstly, there is the
computer database which stores the details of children waiting
and families approved. Secondly, there is a team of experienced
database operators and social workers who will look into the
information that is held and suggest potential matches between
children and prospective adopters.

Local authority adoption agencies will be expected to refer children for whom adoption is the plan three months after this decision has been made, if a local match has not been identified. They must also refer prospective adopters three months after their approval, if they have not already had a child matched with them. Although they are not obliged to do so most voluntary adoption agencies also choose to refer adopters they have approved. All families must give their consent before they can be referred by their agency and can also refer themselves to the Register three months after approval.

Prospective adopters are able to contact Register staff directly for general advice, and to check that they are on referral and that their details are correct. They will be informed if their details have or have not been sent out as a possible link, but they will be advised to contact their social worker for further details about the child or children involved.

Adoption Register for England and Wales
Unit 4, Pavilion Business Park
Royds Hall Road, Wortley
Leeds LS12 6AJ
Tel: 0870 750 2173
Adopters' Helpline: 0870 750 2176
Email: mail@adoptionregister.org.uk
www.adoptionregister.org.uk

Organisations for parents

Adoption UK
Supporting adoptive families
before, during and after
adoption

Adoption UK is a parent-to-parent network of over 3,500 established and potential adoptive families. It welcomes enquiries from prospective adopters; offers local support groups all over the

UK; publishes a wide range of useful leaflets and *Adoption Today* – a bi-monthly magazine written by and for adopters, which also features children waiting for adoption. Current membership rate on request – or visit their website.

Adoption UK
46 The Green
South Bar Street, Banbury
Oxfordshire OX16 9AB
Tel: 01295 752 240
Helpline: 0870 7700 450
Email: admin@adoptionuk.org.uk
www.adoptionuk.org.uk.

AFAA (The Association for Families who have Adopted from Abroad)

A network of families who have adopted from abroad and who offer support and advice to others considering the same.

AFAA
30 Bradgate
Cuttley
Hertfordshire EN6 4RL
Adviceline: 01707 872129
www.afaa.org.uk

Contact a Family

Contact a Family is a national charity for any parent or professional involved with or caring for a child with disabilities. Through a network of mutual support and self-help groups, Contact a Family brings together families whose children have disabilities, and offers advice and information to parents who wish to start a support group.

Contact a Family
209 – 211 City Road
London EC1V 1JN
Tel: 020 7608 8700
Email: info@cafamily.org.uk
Minicom: 020 7608 8702
www.cafamily.org.uk

Post and after adoption centres

There are many well established after adoption services now that provide a service for adoptive families, adopted people and birth parents whose children were adopted. Many of them offer advice and counselling, in person, but also on the telephone or by correspondence, for individuals and families. Some also organise events which focus on matters related to adoption, and provide the opportunity for people to meet in common interest groups.

Post-Adoption Centre
5 Torriano Mews, Torriano Avenue
London NW5 2RZ
Tel: 020 7284 0555
Email: advice@postadoptioncentre.org.uk
www.postadoptioncentre.org.uk

After Adoption
12 – 14 Chapel Street, Salford
Manchester M3 7NH
Tel: 0161 839 4932
Email: administration@afteradoption.org.uk
www.afteradoption.org.uk
After Adoption has a number of regional offices around the UK

After Adoption Yorkshire
31 Moor Road, Headingley
Leeds LS6 4BG

Tel: 0113 230 2100
Emuil: aay@dialstart.net
www.afteradoptionyorkshire.org.uk

Adoption Support (formerly West Midlands Post Adoption Service)
Suite A, 6th Floor
Hurst Street
Birmingham B5 4BD
Tel: 0121 666 6014
Email: wmpasemail@aol.com

Birthlink
Family Care
21 Castle Street
Edinburgh EH2 3DN
Tel: 0131 225 6441
Email: birthlink@charity.vfree.com
www.birthlink.org.uk

Barnardo's Scottish Adoption Advice Service
16 Sandyford Place
Glasgow G3 7NB
Tel: 0141 339 0772
Email: saas@barnardos.org.uk

SWAN (South West Adoption Network)
Leinster House, Leinster Avenue
Knowle
Bristol BS4 1NL
Helpline: 0845 601 2459
Email: helpline@swan-adoption.org.uk
www.swan-adoption.org.uk

Local authorities may also provide help and support. In Scotland, they have a duty to help adoptive families, adopted children and birth families. They sometimes use the help of voluntary agencies for this.

Fostering

Fostering Network (formerly NFCA)

Fostering Network
87 Blackfriars Road
London SE1 8HA
Tel: 020 7620 6400
Email: info@fostering.net
www.fostering.net

Fostering Network (Scotland)

Fostering Network
Ingram House, 2nd Floor
227 Ingram Street
Glasgow G1 1DA
Tel: 0141 204 1400
Email:nfca@fostercare-scotland.org.uk
www.fostercare-scotland.org.uk

Other organisations

Infertility Network UK

Infertility Network UK is the national self-help organisation which provides information, support and representation to people with fertility difficulties and those who work with them.

Membership   £20 per year
£7.50 low income

Infertility Network UK
Charter House
43 St Leonards Road
Bexhill on Sea
East Sussex TN40 1JA
Tel: 01424 732361
Email: admin@infertilitynetworkuk.com
www.infertilitynetworkuk.com

NORCAP – supporting adults affected by adoption

NORCAP is a self-help support group for all parties to adoption.
It offers advice for members on searching and a research service.
It can play an intermediary role for those seeking renewed contact.
NORCAP maintains a successful Contact Register and publishes a
newsletter three times a year.

Initial membership £50 including entry on the Contact Register.

NORCAP
112 Church Road
Wheatley
Oxon OX33 1LU
Tel: 01865 875000
www.norcap.org.uk

Intercountry Adoption Centre

The **Intercountry Adoption Centre** offers advice and information about current policy and practice in relation to overseas adoption and the legal requirements of the UK and "sending" countries. It produces a useful information pack with information about particular countries, and also runs group events.

Intercountry Adoption Centre
64 – 66 High Street
Barnet
Herts EN5 5SJ
Tel: 0870 516 8742
Email: info@icacentre.org.uk
www.icacentre.org.uk

Useful reading

| Books for adults

The Adopter's Handbook
AMY NEIL SALTER
This guide sets out clear, accurate information about adoption before, during and after the big event, to help adopters help themselves throughout the adoption process and beyond. Topics covered include education, health and adoption support.
BAAF 2006 (3rd edition)

Attachment, Trauma and Resilience
KATE CAIRNS
Drawing on Kate's personal experiences with three birth children and 12 fostered children, this book describes family life with children who have experienced attachment difficulties, loss and trauma. Using knowledge and ideas drawn from attachment theory, the author suggests what can be done to promote recovery and develop resilience.
BAAF 2002

Talking about Adoption to your Adopted Child
MARJORIE MORRISON
A guide to the whys, whens, and hows of telling adopted children about their origins.
BAAF 2004 (4th edition)

Adopters on Adoption: Reflections on parenthood and children
DAVID HOWE
In this absorbing collection of personal stories, adoptive parents whose children are now young adults describe the

importance and distinctiveness of adoptive parenting.
BAAF 1996

One of the Family: A handbook for kinship carers
HEDI ARGENT
This handbook aims to give families and friends who may
become kinship carers information about the choices they can
make, the assessment process, legal framework and the
support they can expect.
BAAF 2005

*Looking After our Own: The stories of black and Asian
adopters*
EDITED BY HOPE MASSIAH
An inspiring collection looking at the experiences of nine
black and Asian adoptive families and their children.
BAAF 2005

Could you be my Parent?
EDITED BY LEONIE STURGE-MOORE
This enthralling anthology gathers together a selection of
informative, often moving articles and interviews from *Be My
Parent*, BAAF's family-finding newspaper, to create a
fascinating snapshot of the process of adoption and foster care.
BAAF 2005

*'Just a member of the family': Families and children who
adopt*
BRIDGET BETTS, VIDEO/DVD
This is the first film to look at adoption from a child's point of
view, featuring a number of birth children who have had the
experience of adopting a child into their family.
BAAF 2005

Whatever Happened to Adam? Stories about disabled
children who were adopted or fostered
HEDI ARGENT
This remarkable book tells the stories of 20 young people with
disabilities and the families who chose to care for them.
Following their life journeys from joining their new families,
through childhood and adolescence, it reveals the tremendous
rewards of adopting or fostering a disabled child.
BAAF 1998

First Steps in Parenting the Child who Hurts:
Tiddlers and toddlers (2nd edition)
CAROLINE ARCHER
This book offers practical, sensitive guidance from an
adoptive parent through the areas of separation, loss and
trauma in early childhood which will encourage confidence in
other adoptive parents and foster carers and thereby enable
enjoyment in parenting young children.
Jessica Kingsley Publishers for Adoption UK 1999

Next Steps in Parenting the Child who Hurts: Tykes and
teens
CAROLINE ARCHER
Follows on from the *First Steps* book and shows how love can
be expressed towards the older adopted child, despite
persistent and often extreme tests of that love. Includes a
review of specific sensitive situations that commonly arise and
suggests some solutions.
Jessica Kingsley Publishers for Adoption UK 1999

*The Adoption Experience: Families who give children a
second chance*
ANN MORRIS
Actual adopters tell it like it is on every part of the adoption
process from the exciting moment of first deciding to adopt to
feelings about children seeking a reunion with their natural
families or simply leaving home.
Jessica Kingsley Publishers for Adoption UK in association
with the *Daily Telegraph* 1999

Books for use with children

Nutmeg Gets Adopted
JUDITH FOXON
Nutmeg and his siblings are young squirrels who go into
foster care when their mother finds she cannot keep them safe,
and are then adopted. Beautifully illustrated, this story will
help children in similar situations explore and understand
some of the painful memories they will have of their early life.
Includes practice guidelines.
BAAF 2001

Nutmeg Gets Cross
JUDITH FOXON
This book continues Nutmeg's story by looking at the feelings
that may surface following adoption. This story will help
parents and professionals to understand what may be causing
adopted children to feel cross, confused and sad, and to help
them to heal.
BAAF 2002

Nutmeg Gets a Letter
JUDITH FOXON
The third Nutmeg story looks at contact in adoption, and the
difficulties adopted children may encounter in their feelings

about their birth parents. The helpful role of friendships with other adopted children is also explored. A useful background paper on contact discusses some of the issues.
BAAF 2003

Nutmeg Gets a Little Help
JUDITH FOXON

This book explores the helpful role of adoption support and life story work in helping children to acknowledge and come to terms with their past, and build a sense of self-worth and identity.
BAAF 2004

Nutmeg Gets into Trouble
JUDITH FOXON

Focusing on adopted children in education, this book looks at some common problems they may encounter, from delayed learning to the making of cards for Mother's Day.
BAAF 2006

Adoption: What it is and what it means
SHAILA SHAH

A short, brightly illustrated booklet for children, explaining the process and procedures with short "teaser" questions, quizzes and easy-to-understand definitions of new words.
BAAF 2003

Fostering: What it is and what it means
SHAILA SHAH

This booklet follows a similar format to *Adoption: What it is and what it means* and fulfils a similar need, covering basic information for children about the fostering process.
BAAF 2003

Chester and Daisy Move on
ANGELA LIDSTER
A picture book for 4 – 10-year-olds which tells the story of
two bear cubs that have to leave their family. Work pages are
provided to help children parallel or contrast their own
experiences and feelings.
BAAF 1995

Bruce's Multimedia Story
Bruce is a "spaniel sort of dog" who has to leave his mum and
dad, stay in kennels with his brothers and sisters, and
eventually go to live with a new family.

This electronic resource is designed to capitalise on children's
natural interest in computer-based activities and introduces
animation, music, speech and interactivity. The aim is to make
the experience more interesting and fun for the children and
hence, more productive.
Information Plus 1998

My Life and Me
JEAN CAMIS
This colourful, comprehensive and durable life story work
book can be used flexibly with any child growing up away
from their birth family, including children adopted from
abroad. Includes guidelines to completing the various sections.
BAAF 2001

BAAF children's book series
A unique series of books for use with children separated from
their birth parents. The stories are simply told and attractively
illustrated. Worksheets will help children to compare their
own experiences with those of the story characters.

Living with a New Family: Nadia and Rashid's story (1997)
Nadia is 10 and Rashid seven. When their father died some
years ago, their birth mother, Pat, found it hard to look after
them. So Nadia and Rashid went to live with Jenny, a foster
carer, and then with their new parents, Ayesha and Azeez.

Belonging doesn't Mean Forgetting: Nathan's story (1997)
Nathan is a four-year old African-Caribbean boy and has just
started school. His birth mother, Rose, found it hard to be a
good mum and wanted someone else to look after him. Nathan
went to live with foster carers Tom and Delores, and then with
Marlene, her daughter Sophie, Grannie and Aunty Bea.

Hoping for the Best: Jack's story (1997)
Jack is an eight-year-old white boy whose birth mum couldn't
look after him because she was unhappy and unwell. Jack
went to live with Peter and Sarah. At first he was happy but
then started to feel mixed up. Peter and Sarah did not think
they could be the right parents for him and Jack had to leave.

Feeling Safe: Tina's story (1998)
Tina wasn't safe at home and now lives with Molly who is her
foster carer. Tina had to move after she told a teacher about
how her dad's touches made her feel bad. She is not sure
whether she will ever be able to live with her family again but
feels safe with her foster family.

Joining Together: Jo's story (1998)
Tomorrow will be a big day for eight-year-old Jo. She is going
to court with her mum, stepfather and baby brother to be
adopted. Jo knows that although Dave isn't her birth father he
wants to help look after her for the rest of her life.

| **Advice Notes**

BAAF's popular leaflet series called Advice Notes contains essential information about key areas in adoption and fostering.

Adoption – some questions answered (2006)
Basic information about adoption. Explains the adoption process including the legal issues and the rights of birth parents.

Foster care – some questions answered (2006)
Basic information about fostering. Explains different types of foster care and the relationship with the local authority.

Meeting children's needs through adoption and fostering (2006)
Information for people considering adopting or fostering a child with special needs.

Private fostering (2006)
Aimed at those considering private fostering in England and Wales, this leaflet explains what private fostering involves, and what prospective carers need to know.

Special guardianship (2006)
Provides information about the difference between special guardianship and other forms of permanence for children.

Stepchildren and adoption (2006)
Information for birth parents and step-parents on the advantages or not of adoption, and obtaining further advice. Editions available for England and Wales or Scotland.

Other useful BAAF leaflets

Understanding the assessment process:
information for prospective adopters and carers
A useful leaflet for anyone thinking about applying to offer a
permanent home to a child. It gives a broad overview of what
will be involved in the assessment process.

Intercountry adoption – information and guidance (2006)
Information on adopting a child from overseas, including
procedures, legislation, and where to obtain advice.

Children adopted from abroad: key health and
developmental issues (2004)
Gives advice on the health and medical issues you may
encounter if adopting a child from overseas.

Form ICA
Intercountry adoption form (medical report and development
assessment of child) which, when ordered individually, comes
with two copies of Form AH for the prospective adoptive
parents.

**All the publications listed (with the exception of *Adoption
Today*) are available from BAAF Publications, tel. 020 7421 2604
or visit www.baaf.org.uk.**

Periodicals listing children who need new families

Be My Parent
A UK-wide monthly newspaper for adopters and permanent foster carers who may or may not be approved. It contains features on adoption and fostering and profiles of children across the UK who need new permanent families.
Subscription details available from: 020 7421 2600.

Children in Scotland
As part of the Scottish Resource Network, BAAF Scotland produces a bi-monthly newsletter of children awaiting placement in Scotland. This is distributed to local authorities and voluntary adoption agencies and is available to approved adopters and long-term foster carers.
BAAF Scotland Tel: 0131 220 4749.

Adoption Today
Adoption Today is a monthly journal published by Adoption UK and is available on subscription. It keeps members in touch with one another, profiles children needing new permanent families, and gives information on general developments in the field of adoption.
Adoption UK Tel: 0870 7700 450.

Glossary

Below is a glossary of certain terms that appear in the book. In cases where there is a difference between England and Wales and Scotland, this is shown.

Accommodated/ Accommodation

England and Wales

Under section 20 of the Children Act 1989, the local authority is required to "provide accommodation" for children "in need" in certain circumstances. The local authority does not acquire parental responsibility (see below) merely by accommodating a child and the arrangements for the child must normally be agreed with the parent(s), who, subject to certain circumstances, are entitled to remove the children from local authority accommodation at any time.

Scotland

Under section 25 of the Children (Scotland) Act 1995, the local authority must "provide accommodation" for the children in certain circumstances and may also do so in other situations. Normally, the accommodation is provided by agreement with the parent(s), they can then remove the child at any time in most circumstances. Parental responsibilities remain with the parent(s). A child accommodated under section 25 is a "looked after child" (see below).

Adoption panel

Adoption agencies (local authorities or voluntary adoption societies) are required to set up an adoption panel which must consider and make recommendations on children for whom adoption is the plan, on prospective adopters and on matches between prospective adopters and children.

Adoption placement plan

A term used in England. A plan that gives information to the prospective adopter about the child when the agency has decided to place the child with them. It sets out, for example, when the child will move into the prospective adopter's home, parental responsibility, adoption support services, contact with the child, and arrangements for reviewing the placement.

Adoption placement report

A term used in England. A report prepared by the adoption agency for the adoption panel which sets out, for example, the reasons for proposing the placement, arrangement for allowing any person contact with the child, the prospective adopter's view on the proposed placement, and, where the agency is a local authority, proposals for providing adoption support services for the adoptive family.

Adoption Register

A database of approved prospective adopters and children waiting for adoption across England and Wales. A team of experienced social workers will use the database to link children with approved prospective adopters where local matches cannot be found.

Adoption Support Agency (ASA)

An organisation or person registered, under Part 2 of the Care Standards Act 2000, to provide adoption support services. An ASA may operate on a profit or not-for-profit basis.

Annex A report

A court report in relation to an adoption application in England.

Article 15 report

A report prepared on the prospective adopter under Article 15 of the Convention on Protection of Children and Co-operation in respect of

Intercountry Adoption (the Hague Convention). This includes
information on their identity, eligibility and suitability to adopt,
background, family and medical history, social environment, reasons
for adoption, ability to undertake an intercountry adoption and the
characteristics of the children for whom they would be qualified to
care.

| Article 16 information

A report prepared on the child under Article 16 of the Hague
Convention. This includes information on his/her identity,
adoptability, background, social environment, family history,
medical history including that of the child's family, and any special
needs of the child.

| CAFCASS

The Children and Family Court Advisory and Support Service is a
national non-departmental public body for England. It has brought
together the services provided by the Family Court Welfare Service,
the Guardian *ad Litem* Services and the Children's Division of the
Official Solicitor. CAFCASS is independent of the courts, social
services, education and health authorities and all similar agencies.
A CAFCASS officer must formally witness the consent to adoption
of a birth parent.

| CAMHS (Child and Adolescent Mental Health Services)

Services that contribute to the mental health care of children and
young people, whether provided by health, education or social
services or other agencies. CAMHS cover all types of provision and
intervention from mental health promotion and primary prevention,
specialist community-based services.

| **Care Order**

Applies only to England and Wales. A child who is subject to a Care Order is described as being "in care". A Care Order gives the local authority parental responsibility for the child but does not deprive the parent(s) of this. Nevertheless, the local authority may limit the extent to which parents may exercise their parental responsibility and may override parental wishes in the interests of the child's welfare.

| **Children's guardian**

Applies only to England and Wales. A person appointed by the court to safeguard a child's interests in court proceedings (formerly called a guardian *ad litem*). Local authorities are required to establish panels of people to act as children's guardians in care proceedings and in adoption proceedings. Their duties are set out in court rules and include presenting a report to the court.

| **Consortium**

A group of usually not more than six – eight local adoption agencies, often both local authorities and voluntary adoption agencies, who share details of waiting families and children in order to try and make speedy local placements for children.

| **Contact/Contact Order**

England and Wales

Contact may be used to mean visits, including residential visits or other form of direct face-to-face contact between a child and another individual, or it may mean indirect ways of keeping in touch, e.g. letters or telephone calls including letters sent via a third party. Once a local authority is authorised to place a child for adoption, there is no presumption for or against contact. The child's needs will be the paramount consideration.

Scotland

As in England and Wales, contact can mean direct or indirect contact or access. It covers private arrangements (e.g. in divorce, etc), it also covers a public law situation when a child is "looked after" by a local authority. When a child is on a supervision requirement (see above) under the Children's Hearing system, the hearing regulates contact.

| Curator *ad litem*

Similar to children's guardian in England and Wales (see above).

| Fostering/foster care

In this book this term is used for those cases where a child is placed with a foster carer approved by the local authority and/or placed directly by a voluntary organisation. These placements are governed by the Fostering Services Regulations 2002 in England and by the Fostering of Children (Scotland) Regulations 1996 in Scotland. "Short-term", "long-term" and "permanent" foster care and "respite care" may mean different things to different people – they are not legally defined terms.

| Freeing Order/freeing for adoption

England and Wales
A Freeing Order under the Adoption Act 1976 ends parents' parental responsibility and transfers parental responsibility to the adoption agency. The purpose of this is to allow any issue regarding parental consent to adoption to be resolved before the child is placed with prospective adopters. In certain circumstances the "former parent" may ask the court to revoke the order if the child is not placed with prospective adopters after one year. Freeing orders can no longer be applied for (from 30 December 2005) but existing freeing orders remain in force and authorise the local authority to place a child for adoption.

Scotland
A Freeing Order under the Adoption (Scotland) Act 1978 has the same effect as above. It is an optional court process by a local authority before an application for adoption.

| Guardian

A guardian is a person who has been formally appointed as a child's guardian after the death of one or both parents. The appointment may be made in writing by a parent or by a court.

| Independent Review
| Mechanism (IRM)

This is only available to people assessed by an adoption agency in England, and is a review process that is conducted by an independent review panel. The prospective adopter may initiate this process when their adoption agency has made a qualifying determination. The review panel reviews the case and gives a fresh recommendation to the agency.

| Looked after

England and Wales
This term includes both children "in care" and accommodated children. Local authorities have certain duties towards all looked after children and their parents, which are set out in Part III of the Children Act 1989. These include the duty to safeguard and promote the child's welfare and the duty to consult with children and parents before taking decisions.

Scotland
This term covers all children for whom the local authority has responsibilities under section 17 of the Children (Scotland) Act 1995. It replaces the term "in care". It is wider than and different from the English and Welsh definition. It includes children who remain at home as well as those placed away from home.

| Open adoption

This term may be used very loosely and can mean anything from an adoption where a child continues to have frequent face-to-face contact with members of his or her birth family to an adoption where there is some degree of "openness", e.g. the birth family and adopters meeting each other once. People using the term should be asked to define what they mean!

| **Parental responsibility**

England and Wales

This is defined in the Children Act 1989 as 'all the rights, duties, powers and responsibilities which by law a parent has in relation to a child and his property'. When a child is born to married parents, they will both share parental responsibility for him or her, and this parental responsibility can never be lost except on the making of an Adoption Order. A father who is not married to the child's mother does not automatically have parental responsibility but may acquire it either by formal agreement with the mother or by court order. Adoptive parents in England and Wales acquire parental responsibility when a child is placed with them, although the local authority placing the child can restrict their exercise of this until the adoption order is made.

Parental responsibilities and rights – Scotland

These are what parents have for their children and are defined in sections 1 and 2 of the Children (Scotland) Act 1995. All mothers have them automatically; fathers only if married to the mother at conception or later. However, fathers can get them by formal agreement with the mother or by a court order.

Anyone can go to court for an order about parental responsibilities and rights under section 11 of the Children (Scotland) Act 1995. Residence Orders (see below) and Contact Orders (see above) are examples. The court can also take away responsibilities and rights under this section.

Parents or others with responsibilities and rights can only lose them by a court order: an Adoption Order, Parental Responsibilities Order (see below), or an order under section 11.

In relation to a father who is not married to the mother, the father can obtain these rights through an agreement under the Children (Scotland) Act 1995.

Parental Responsibilities Order

A term used in Scotland. This section removes all parental responsibility from the parent(s) (except the right to consent (or not) to adoption) and gives them to the local authority. It is granted under section 86 of the Children (Scotland) Act 1995.

Placement order

An order made by the court under section 21 of the Adoption and Children Act 2002 authorising a local authority to place a child for adoption with any prospective adopters who may be chosen by the authority. It continues in force until it is revoked, or an adoption order is made in respect of the child, or the child marries, forms a civil partnership or attains the age of 18. Only local authorities may apply for placement orders.

Qualifying determination

A term used in England. In relation to *suitability to adopt a child* – a determination is made by an adoption agency that it considers a prospective adopter is not suitable to be an adoptive parent and does not propose to approve him/her as suitable to be an adoptive parent.

Reporting officer

A member of the panel of curators *ad litem* and reporting officers, appointed by the court for adoption proceedings. His or her specific task is to ensure that the agreement of a parent or guardian to an Adoption Order, if given, is given freely and with full understanding of what is involved and to witness the agreement.

| Residence Order

England and Wales

An order under the Children Act 1989 settling the arrangements as to the person/s with whom the child is to live. Where a Residence Order is made in favour of someone who does not already have parental responsibility for the child (e.g. a relative or foster carer), that person will acquire parental responsibilities subject to certain restrictions (e.g. they will not be able to consent to the child's adoption). Parental responsibility given in connection with a Residence Order will only last as long as the Residence Order. A Residence Order normally only lasts until the child's 16th birthday.

Scotland

This is one of the orders possible under section 11 of the Children (Scotland) Act 1995. It regulates with whom the child lives. If the person with the Residence Order did not have any parental responsibilities and rights before, the order gives those as well.

| Residence Order
| allowance

England and Wales

Local authorities have a power to contribute to the cost of a child's maintenance when the child is living with somebody under a Residence Order provided he or she is not living with a parent or step-parent. A financial contribution under this power is normally referred to as a Residence Order allowance.

Scotland

Local authorities have the power to pay an allowance to a person who has care of a child and who is not a parent or a foster carer. The person does not have to have a Residence Order.

Section 23 or section 22 reports

Applies only to Scotland. Reports to the court are under section 23 in agency adoptions and section 22 in non-agency cases, e.g. step-parents, of the Adoption (Scotland) Act 1978. The Rules of Court give guidance about what should be in the reports.

Special guardianship

A new order in England and Wales under the Adoption and Children Act 2002 offering an alternative legal status for children. The child is no longer looked after. It gives the special guardian parental responsibility which he or she can exercise to the exclusion of others. However, the birth parent(s) retain parental responsibility. Support services, including financial support, are very similar to those for adopters.

Supervision requirements

Applies only to Scotland. These are the orders made by the Children's Hearing for any child needing compulsory measures of supervision. Children may be victims of abuse or neglect, have other problems and/or have committed crimes. All children on supervision requirements are "looked after" by the local authority, even if they live at home. Supervision requirements do not give parental responsibilities and rights to local authorities.

Books on adoption from BAAF

Looking after our own

The stories of black and Asian adopters

Edited by Hope Massiah

This inspiring collection looks at the experiences of nine adoptive families and their children. Essential reading for anyone considering adopting a child, especially those from minority ethnic communities.

£9.95   132 PAGES 126 X 194MM   ISBN 1 903699 70 3

Could you be my parent?

Adoption and fostering stories

Edited by Leonie Sturge-Moore

Accounts taken from BAAF's family-finding newspaper *Be My Parent* of children who needed a new permanent family and the people who welcomed them into their homes.

£8.50   182 PAGES 126 X 194MM   ISBN 1 903699 82 7

Approaching fatherhood

A guide for adoptive dads and others

Paul May

An adoptive dad describes how men can become fathers by adoption. In the first book-length treatment of the subject, Paul May offers challenging observations on the nature of fatherhood today.

£9.95   173 PAGES A5   ISBN 1 903699 65 7

Talking about adoption to your adopted child

A guide for adoptive parents

Marjorie Morrison

Packed with practical ideas for talking to children of all ages, including those with disabilities and those from a different ethnic background, this book gives information on tracing birth parents, useful organisations and further reading.

£7.50   150 PAGES 126 X 194MM   ISBN 1 903699 52 5

Order online at www.baaf.org.uk or by phoning BAAF Publications on 020 7421 2604 or emailing pubs.sales@baaf.org.uk.

Registered charity number 275689

Be My Parent can help!

Be My Parent aims to raise awareness about adoption and fostering, recruit new families and link children with permanent families.

About Be My Parent:

- a newspaper, published every month, featuring hundreds of children needing new, permanent families from all over the UK
- information on adoption and fostering, and lively interviews and articles
- help with liaising between social workers and prospective families

Please get in touch if you would like to find out more about our services, talk in confidence about adoption and fostering, receive a free information pack (including a sample of profiles and a list of adoption and fostering agencies in your area), purchase an introductory copy or subscribe to *Be My Parent.*

Be My Parent, BAAF
Saffron House, 6–10 Kirby Street, London EC1N 8TS
Telephone: 020 7421 2666
Email: bmp@baaf.org.uk
www.baaf.org.uk